The Call of Darkness

A Relational Listening Approach to Suicide Intervention

Lawrence Hedges

Listening Perspectives Press
ORANGE, California
2018 / 2023

Cover Design: Afton Palmer

To my husband
Daniel Uribe,
who for more than a decade has provided Love,
support, and encouragement for our lives
and for my work.

Acknowledgements

The massive research effort that this book represents owes its impetus to a great support team that has worked diligently sorting through more than fifty books and two hundred articles to bring this amazing distillation to you.

Gratitude goes to Monica Mello, Lynn Connors, Ray Calabrese, Daniel Uribe, and Breta Hedges. Also I owe a debt of extreme gratitude to my publisher, Jason Aronson, who saw the promise of my work as early as 1981 and has carefully guided my work and offered support and enthusiasm ever since. Thanks to Melonie Bell, whose painstaking editing has made possible nine electronic books on the free download website of the International Psychotherapy Institute (freepsychotherapybooks.org). And thanks to Greggory Moore (greggorymoore.com), who edited the final version of this book.

Table of Contents

Author's Preface

I am a psychologist-psychoanalyst who for 45 years has been in private practice specializing in training and supervising psychotherapists and psychoanalysts on their most difficult cases. Recently I published *Relational Listening: A Handbook: Cross-Culturally Resonate Gateways into Human Relational Experience*, the 20th book in a series that surveys a massive clinical research project extending over the 45 years and participated in by more than 400 psychotherapists in case conferences, reading groups and seminars at the Listening Perspectives Study Center and the Newport Psychoanalytic Institute in the Southern California area.

Over the years I have consulted on literally thousands of perplexing and difficult-to-treat cases brought to me individually and in case conference groups by professional colleagues and trainees—nationally and internationally. More recently I have a Zoom HIPAA-compliant platform and am doing distant video consulting on difficult-to-treat cases and cases involving suicidality. These books have been paralleled by Continuing Education classes for Mental Health Professionals, many of which have been video recorded and are available through YouTube links on my website, ListeningPerspectives.com, as well as sfrankelgroup.com.

My impetus for in-depth research on the topic of suicide was a 2017 mandate from the California Board of Psychology that all licensed psychologists shall take a six-hour Continuing Education course in Suicide Prevention. This mandate came down from the Obama White House spurred on by numerous national health organizations declaring an epidemic in suicides, especially among young people. The mandate went down through governor's offices and is slowly being passed down to state licensing boards for health professionals nationally. Since continuing education for mental health professionals has been a longtime specialty of mine, I took the challenge to begin researching every book and article on suicide I could get my hands on—a search fortunately made easier these days by Amazon as well as web journal subscriptions.

I quickly came to the impression that the topic of suicide is the most widely considered and studied phenomena of human experience. All cultural groups since the beginning of recorded time have had to come to grips with suicide in one way or another. Suicide has interested philosophers, theologians, judges, poets and artists for thousands of years—only to be followed in recent centuries by sociologists, anthropologists, and psychologists. In this book I will report what I consider to be some of the highlights of my research into what is now rapidly coming to be seen as a global crisis of epidemic proportions.

Shockingly, after all this scholarly and artistic attention over such a long period of time no widely agreed upon theories of suicide have emerged and virtually all the efforts to predict and prevent suicide have yielded results no better than chance.[1]

---

[1] Franklin et al. (2016). "Risk Factors for Suicidal Thoughts and Behaviors: A Meta-Analysis of 50 Years of Research," by Joseph Franklin, PhD, and Jessica Ribeiro, PhD, Vanderbilt University and Harvard University; Kathryn Fox, AM, Evan Kleinman, PhD, Adam Jaroszewski, AM, and Matthew Nock, PhD, Harvard University; Kate Bentley, MA, Boston University; Xieyining Huang, BA, and Katherine Musacchio, MEd, Vanderbilt University; and Bernard Chang, MD, Columbia University. *Psychological Bulletin*, published online Nov. 14, 2016.

However, some groups of practicing therapists have recently developed various approaches that seem to point to a hopeful direction and I will survey those for you.

But most puzzling to me as I considered the epidemic proportions of suicidality, and the reported ineffectiveness of prediction and prevention was that in 45 years of practicing and supervising cases of hundreds of therapists and literally thousands of clients we have experienced not one suicide! Oh, we have worked through countless instances of suicidality to be sure—troubling threats and gestures, as well as all kinds of parasuicidal and high-risk behaviors—but not one death. I did report one suicide of a man who had been in treatment with an intern I was consulting with who at the end of her internship was forced by personal circumstances to terminate and transfer him. The transfer was made to an experienced therapist not in consultation with me and was very carefully handled. But despite careful planning the man was dead in a few months. The three of us, my intern, the treating therapist and myself did conduct a "postvention" study that was extremely revealing and was published.[2] The bottom line was that a deep maternal transference of hope had been established with the intern that the severely troubled man was unable to transfer to the new therapist and the deep rupture of a reenacted abandonment in infancy precipitated the bullet in the head.

So why, with suicides escalating nationally and world-wide have the therapists involved in our research and consultation project not experienced a single death in the numerous cases we

---

[2] In Hedges (1994).

have been treating and consulting with together? Certainly we had the consultative expertise of Norman Farbarow available for many years that helped us through a number of tough spots. But how have we (so far!) made it safely through? I hope the answer to this question slowly becomes clear as we consider suicide from a Relational Listening perspective and as we consider the promising work of several other groups of professional therapists who, with very different theories and techniques, are experiencing successes too. There are some things we must all be doing in common to help people through unbearable anguish—what is it exactly? Poet Edward Arlington Robinson long ago mused on this question:

Richard Cory

Whenever Richard Cory went downtown,
We people on the pavement looked at him:
He was a gentleman from sole to crown,
Clean favored, and imperially slim.

And he was always quietly arrayed,
And he was always human when he talked;
But still he fluttered pulses when he said,
"Good-morning," and he glittered when he walked.

And he was rich—yes, richer than a king—
And admirably schooled in every grace:
In fine, we thought that he was everything
To make us wish that we were in his place.

So on we worked, and waited for the light,
And went without the meat, and cursed the bread;
And Richard Cory, one calm summer night,
Went home and put a bullet through his head.

Why did he...? What made her...?

What about the family, her children...? Who would have suspected...?

I saw him just yesterday—There was no indication...!

Not a word from her...!

Why didn't he ask for help...? I'm really hurting...

I'm really angry...! I'm totally perplexed. Why, why, why...?

These are the questions people have been asking since the beginning of time and I hope to demonstrate in this book that none of these "why and wherefore" questions will help us at all in getting to the heart of what suicidality is all about. At this point in time we have to step back and carefully reconsider suicidality in light of recent advances in infant research, neuroscience, anthropology, sociology, and psychotherapy on the relational nature of our species and the ways our human minds are formed, transformed, and passed on to our children.

Introduction

There are ten, and only ten, definitive statements that can be made about suicide that most experts around the world can agree upon. In the course of this book I will elaborate on each of these key statements.

1. **Suicidality is complex, idiosyncratic, and relational.** It is not a singularity—a something to be clearly defined and categorized. Nor is suicidality a pathological dimension that can be rated from mild to moderate to severe. Despite the frequent appearance of being isolated and alone, suicidality invariably includes an implicit or explicit relationship or set of relationships.

2. **Ambivalence is detectable in all forms of suicidality—** No matter how apparently resolute the suicide act appears. Further, in a "suicide autopsy" there are always indications, clues, and pointers that constitute "a cry for help" or "a cry of pain"—clues that were missed at the time.

3. **All social and cultural groups since the beginning of time have known and have had to deal with suicide—** with radically different results depending on the specific era and the cultural context.

4. **Suicide is an exclusively human behavior and is therefore an activity of the human *mind*—**with significant psychosomatic consequences. There are no established suicide genes, neurons, or neurotransmitters.

5. **"Psycheache" is the mind/body agony associated with suicidal experiences.** The intervention questions are: "Tell me where it hurts?" and "How can I help you." Both of these questions open up an intersubjective, collaborative search for the personal meanings involved in the psycheache.

6. **The population of people who successfully complete suicide is decidedly different from the populations of attempters and ideationers**—though accidents sometimes make for a small overlap. Therefore, ideas taken from the populations of attempters and ideationers cannot be used to understand those fully intent on suicide, the completers—other formulations are necessary.

7. **All completed suiciders and many attempters and ideationists have been or could have been at one time diagnosed with a severe or borderline mental disorder**—major depression, bipolar, schizophrenia, and anxiety disorder as well as PTSD, borderline, schizoid, sociopathic and narcissistic character disorders.

8. **Massive research over more than a century has produced no widely agreed-upon theories of suicidality.**

9. **There are no consistently reliable and empirically validated ways to predict or treat suicide.**

10. **Over time groups of psychotherapists have developed some ways of working with suicidality that seem promising.**

My thesis: **A Relational Listening approach that explains how past relational traumas impact current relational contexts can shed fresh light on the many issues surrounding suicidality.**

Throughout the suicide literature countless experts and suicidality experiencers repeatedly point to the earliest eras of life as having somehow been formative in how suicidality manifests later in life. Losses, rejections, abandonments, and abuse in early in life are usually seen as the culprits—but since all people have experienced loss, rejection, and abandonment, what kinds of experiences—in what contexts and at what developmental junctures—may pave the way for serious suicidality later in life? And how do traumas in later life "telescope" or collapse downward the magnitude of their impact to early infant trauma? Furthermore, since the countless consciously and socially constructed narratives of suicidal behavior attesting to various causes and motives—such as a cry for help or pain or a friend or loved one's manipulation—seem to offer little or no help to those in the throes of suicidal anguish, observers are inclined to invoke the idea of unconscious and unformulated motives based on traumatic experiences that happened too early in life to be remembered in ordinary ways. Here the psychoanalysts may have something to offer.

Sigmund Freud was the first to assert that traumatic experience that cannot be consciously remembered must be enacted in later relational situations.[3] His notion of unconscious experience that was retrievable in therapy was based on a five-

---

[3] S. Freud (1914).

year-old's capacity to narrate, to symbolize and to repressively self-instruct ideas and experiences to disappear from consciousness. It was psychoanalyst Christopher Bollas who first pointed to the unconscious of the "unthought known"—memories that have been stored in pre-verbal somatic and affective interactional modes that had never been subjected to thought until in the therapy relationship the enactments can be lived, experienced and framed in conscious thought.[4] The Interpersonal/Relational psychoanalysts Edgar Levenson, Philip Bromberg, and Donnel Stern, basing their work on Harry Stack Sullivan's insights from his work with schizophrenics, came to speak of "unformulated experience" that is, somatic and affective memories formed in earliest relationships that are repeatedly enacted in relationships until in a therapeutic relationship the dissociation from consciousness could be bridged and two could come to talk about the mutual enactments that stem from early pre-verbal and pre-symbolic experience.[5] Intersubjective psychoanalyst Robert Stolorow and his colleagues speak of the "pre-reflective unconscious" as an aspect of relational experience that can become known in an intersubjectively-oriented therapy.[6] The Listening Perspectives group I am a part of has devised a series of Relational Listening perspectives for framing different developmental forms of unconscious experience—whether repressed, dissociated, unformulated or unintegrated.[7]

---

[4] Bollas (1987).

[5] Levenson (2016); Bromberg (2011); Stern (2003); Sullivan (1970).

[6] Stolorow et al. (1980).

[7] Hedges, *Listening Perspectives in Psychotherapy* (1983, 2003) and *Relational Listening* (2018).

I would like to begin our adventure into the complex labyrinth of suicidality by introducing the Relational Listening approach that was not originally devised to deal with suicidality, but rather evolved to help therapists and their clients tune into life's earliest traumatic experiences. It was only as I turned my research spotlight on suicidality that I came to realize that the Relational Listening approach that targets and allows a here-and-now therapeutic unpacking or re-living of primal emotional relatedness experience can provide the theory and intersubjective approach that suicidologists have been searching so long for.

Chapter One

The Relational Listening Approach

Since I will be introducing a Relational Listening way of considering suicidality and interventions to be used with people who declare themselves in one way or another to be suicidal, I will give a rough sketch of the approach at the beginning to give you an idea of where I will be going; but I must leave fuller explanations until later when, in the context of case and film illustrations, they will make more sense.

A century of psychoanalytic research has yielded four main watersheds of relational development—each with its own relational fears. Anyone subjected to overwhelming neglect, abuse, terror, intimidation, or shame during any one of the earliest phases of life is vulnerable to having similar overwhelming levels of fear, constriction, and/or fragmentation triggered by intimate relationships and/or perceived interpersonal demands later in life. What follows is a summary chart and a brief narrative of the relational issues and relational fears involved. These relational experiences and fears will be used later in an attempt to make sense of various kinds of suicidal behavior.

Four Developmental Listening Experiences and Seven Relational Fears

I. The Organizing experience
   (approximately ± 4 months after birth)

  1. The fear of being alone

  2. The fear of making connections

II. The Symbiotic experience
   (4-24 months)

3. The fear of abandonment

4. The fear of self-assertion

III. The Selfother experience
   (24 to 36 months)

    5. The fear of being unacceptable

IV. The Independent experience
   (36 months through adolescence)

    6. The fear of failure and success

    7. The fear of being fully alive

A person could experience focal or cumulative trauma in relationships at any stage of life and need to re-experience that trauma in a later therapeutic relationship in order to work through the post-traumatic experiences that are still creating problems.[8] That is, *relational traumas from the past tend to re-assert themselves—transfer into—the context of current intimate relationships and perceived interpersonal demands. But truly terrifying and deeply traumatic experiences that impact the fundamental ways the personality organizes itself are more characteristic of the earliest stages of development—the "Organizing" and the "Symbiotic" relational experiences.*

The Relational Listening point of view predicts that *seriously intentional suicides* are re-enactments from trauma experienced at the Organizing level of experience. And that most other *suicide attempts and self-harm behaviors* derive from trauma at the Symbiotic level of experience. On the other hand, various *suicidal ideations and high-risk behaviors* are attributable to the higher "Self-other" and "Independent" or "neurotic/normal" layers of

---

[8] Hedges (2015).

relational experience which may call for interpersonal empathy but no serious intervention. There are crucial interpersonal implications of this point of view for intervention in these various levels of relational complexity.

Here is a brief sketch of what each of these experiences and fears looks like.[9] Since most of our concern with suicidality and interventions revolves around traumas in the first two levels of relational development—levels that are preverbal and pre-symbolic—I will focus in this book mostly on issues at these levels of relational complexity and only briefly attend to the levels of greater relational complexity involving suicide ideation, parasuicidal behaviors, and high-risk behaviors. It is important at this point for you to spend a few minutes getting the idea of each of these early experiences and fears clear in your mind because the illustrative cases throughout the book will be analyzed mostly in terms of these first two Relational Listening experiences and fears.

I feel it important to clarify here that these experiences and fears—while presented as almost developmental stages are more properly thought of as *metaphors* based on relational development and are first and foremost definitions of Listening Perspectives—that is, ways that we can listen to someone's life experiences. These categories are thus properly understood as a dimension of human relatedness potentials—potentials that we all engage in in various ways throughout our days—that can be "listened to" in the broadest possible sense while engaged in an intimate relationship.

---

[9] I have elaborated these experiences and fears and illustrated them extensively with case studies in Hedges (2012b, 2013a,c, 2015, 2018).

When used as perspectives from which a person in an interpersonal relational situation can momentarily grasp the kinds of relatedness currently in play, they can be immensely helpful as the many case studies authored by many different therapists in my books demonstrate. That is, all of my work specifically eschews the idea that we can ever definitively know what is going on in the human mind since mind is interactional, culturally and linguistically determined, ever-changing, and replete with infinite possibilities. Theories that define or name mental structures or purport stages of development are still participating in an outmoded "modernist" epistemology of seventeenth century objectively-oriented science. In contrast, the Listening Perspective schema offers a "post-modern" approach with perspectives constructed to organize in one's mind an infinity of relational possibilities.

I. THE ORGANIZING EXPERIENCE

Infants require certain forms of connection and inter-connection in order to remain psychologically alert and enlivened to themselves and to others. In their early relatedness they are busy "Organizing" physical and mental channels of connection—first to mother's body and later to her mind and to the minds of others—for nurturance, stimulation, soothing, and evacuation. Traumas of over- or under-stimulation leave harsh marks on the developing mind that may or may not be detectable until they are transferred into later relatedness experiences. Framing Organizing patterns of relational trauma for therapy entails studying how two people approach to make connections and then turn away, veer off, rupture, or dissipate the intensity of the connections.

1. The Fear of Being Alone

We dread reaching out and finding nobody there to respond to our needs. We fear being ignored, being left alone, and being seen as unimportant. We feel the world does not respond to our needs. So what's the use of trying?

2. The Fear of Interpersonally Connecting

Because of frightening and painful experiences with caregiving others in the distant past, connecting emotionally and intimately with others feels perennially dangerous. Our life experiences have left us feeling that the world is not a safe place. We fear injury so we avoid and withdraw from potential interpersonal connections.

II. THE SYMBIOTIC EXPERIENCE

Toddlers are busy learning how to make emotional relationships (both good and bad) work for them. They experience a sense of merger and reciprocity with their primary caregivers, thus establishing many knee-jerk, automatic, *character*ological, and role-reversible patterns or scenarios of relatedness that are unique to each bonding pair. Framing the trauma-based symbiotic relatedness patterns for therapy entails noting how each person *character*istically engages the other and how interactive scenarios evolve from two subjectively-formed sets of internalized self-and-other interaction patterns. That is, in a symbiotically engaged pair each *instrumentally* manipulates the other in sequences of mutual affect regulation.

3. The Fear of Being Abandoned

After having connected emotionally or bonded with someone, we fear being either abandoned with our own needs or being swallowed up by the other person's needs. In either case, we feel the world is not a dependable place and that we live in danger of rejection and emotional abandonment. We may become clingy and dependent, or we may become super independent—or both.

4. The Fear of Self-Assertion

We have all experienced rejection, and perhaps even punishment and shame for expressing ourselves in a way that others don't like. We thus may learn to fear asserting ourselves and letting our needs be known in relationships. We feel the world does not allow us to be truly ourselves. We may either cease putting ourselves out there altogether, or we may assert ourselves with demanding vengeance.

III. THE SELF-OTHER[10] EXPERIENCE

Two- and three-year-olds are preoccupied with using the acceptance and approval of others for developing and enhancing self-definitions, self-skills, and self-esteem. Their relatedness strivings use the mirroring, twinning,

---

[10] Heinz Kohut's original term was "selfobject."

and idealizing responses of significant others to firm up their budding sense of self. Framing for therapy the self-other patterns used for affirming, confirming, and inspiring the self entails studying how the internalized mirroring, twinning, and idealizing patterns used in self development in the pasts of both participants play out to enhance and limit the possibilities for mutual self-to-self-other resonance in the emerging interpersonal engagement.

5. The Fear of Lack of Recognition

When we do not get the acceptance and confirmation we need in relationships and interpersonal settings, we are left with a feeling of not being seen or recognized for whom we really are. Or, we may fear that others will only respect and love us if we are who they want us to be. We may work continuously to feel seen and recognized by others, or we may give up in rage, humiliation, or shame.

IV. THE INDEPENDENCE EXPERIENCE

Four- to seven-year-olds are dealing with triangular love and hate relationships and are moving toward more complex social relationships. In their relatedness they experience others as separate centers of initiative and themselves as independent agents in a socially competitive and cooperative environment. Framing the internalized patterns of independently-interacting selves in both cooperative and competitive triangulations with real and fantasized third parties experienced in childhood and again in adolescence entails studying the emerging interaction patterns for evidence of repressive forces operating within each participant and between the therapeutic couple that work to limit or spoil the full interactive potential.

6. The Fear of Failure and Success

When we have loved and lost or tried and failed, we may fear painful competitive experiences. When we have succeeded or won—possibly at someone else's expense—we may experience guilt or fear retaliation. Thus, we learn to hold back in love and life, thereby not risking either failure or success. In our conflicts we may feel the world does not allow us to be fulfilled. Or we may feel guilty and afraid for feeling fulfilled.

7. The Fear of Being Fully Alive

Our expansiveness, creative energy, and joy in our aliveness inevitably come into conflict with family, work, religion, and society. We come to believe that we must curtail our aliveness to conform to the expectations and demands of the world. We feel the world does not permit us to be fully, joyfully, and passionately alive. Rather than putting our whole selves out there with full energy, we may throw in the towel, succumb to mediocre conformity, or fall into living deadness.

In Relational forms of psychotherapy we expect that it will be only a matter of time before the scars of preverbal, pre-symbolic, unformulated traumas of early childhood will re-assert themselves, that is, be repeated in the therapeutic relationship. Let's consider how the Organizing and Symbiotic experiences can transfer and become manifest in various forms of suicidality.

The transfer from an *Organizing experience* trauma is recognizable in a shutting down, a blocking, or a switching of attention at moments when empathic connection between therapist and client are about to be or have been successfully made. That is, early trauma is experienced in the context of an infant reaching out for satisfaction—and instead experiencing traumatic emptiness or hurt. When the potentially satisfying connection is somehow painfully thwarted the infant learns that to connect—to long for competence in connecting to others, to oneself, and to the interpersonal world—is dangerous. Thus the refusal, blocking, or backing away from connections in intimate and trust relationships points to the nature of the original scar. And when the nature of the original contact is actually abusive or injurious all the more reason to "never reach that way again." Metaphorically, one turns from the light of consciousness (i.e., knowing together) toward the call of darkness of safe retreat, of rest, of the peace to be found in the unconsciousness of sleep and death. At moments of helplessness, hopelessness, and despair in later life others may experience the person as depressed, bipolar, anxious, autistic or whatever. *It is my belief that successfully intentioned suicides are rooted in this kind of transfer from a traumatic infancy experience into a current interpersonally demanding or potentially rewarding relationship or social situation—no matter how otherwise well developed, intelligent or creative the individual may be.* I will fully illustrate this later. Said differently, just at the point that some potentially powerful and affirming connection arises in a relationship or interpersonal social situation the person—transferring an organizing experience

29

fear—will experience an inner retreat or collapse of some sort—i.e., is liable to "snatch defeat from the jaws of success"—through backing away from or thwarting full affective connection through "psychotic symptoms" of one sort or another. This is certainly the call of darkness. Note that people with active or chronic diagnosable serious mental illnesses are perennially experiencing this level of relatedness experience with an array of ways of avoiding, thwarting, or withdrawing from interpersonal connections (so-called "symptoms"). On the other hand many deeply traumatized individuals may move forward into normal and even extraordinary adult life experiences and achievements, but when some relational experience is over-stimulating (i.e., potentially fulfilling or successful in certain ways) it can easily trigger the inner retreat or collapse into darkness. Certainly at that moment there is a psychotic failure of ordinary consensual reality testing operating.

Alternatively, the transfer from the *Symbiotic* experience manifests in therapy when prior connecting or attaching experiences have been reliably successful, and an infant is able to engage in a certain set of relationship scenarios involving mutual affect regulation and mutual instrumental manipulations with caregivers so that a bonding or attachment style becomes possible. Those infants and toddlers that form "secure" attachments are able to move toward individuation and more complex levels of relational possibilities (i.e., the selfother and independence forms of relating). However, those infants and toddlers that develop "insecure" attachments form enduring bonding patterns that either cling too closely to mother or conversely withdraw from closeness with her. Every bonding couple has its own "mommy and me are one" set of satisfactions and frustrations according to a certain style or engagement mode that is unique to each couple. This uniqueness is why "borderline" or "character" pathology is always idiosyncratic and—despite diagnostic attempts—cannot be clearly specified in advance as to what exactly it looks like.

If all goes well in the second year of life and a "secure" attachment or bonding set of experiences has been established, then a separation-individuation from the established bonding pattern is set to occur with the infant refusing Mommy's way and the Mother allowing (or not) the tantrums and opposition to free the child from symbiotic bondage. But often enough in "insecure" forms of attachment this psychological differentiation fails to occur or may only partially occur. The person may continue to develop well in many ways, but the person remains stuck with a somewhat restricted or rigid character style (so-called "borderline," "sociopathic," "narcissistic," etc.). Later in life, and re-enacted in therapy, this restricted or instrumental character style may be experienced by others as manipulative, coercive, demanding, constricting, alienating, or self-limiting. That is, the person who did not achieve a "secure" attachment followed by personal individuation may be experienced by others as needing or demanding relatedness that is (unconsciously) intended to be instrumental in molding relationships into his/her accustomed relatedness needs and styles irrespective of the other's boundaries and needs. Suicide threats and gestures as well as "parasuicidal" (self-injury) behaviors may be engaged in with the (usually unconscious) hope of somehow impacting others so that one's conscious or unconscious symbiotic relatedness (dependency) needs and habits can be met.

Aside on Relatedness Potentials

I want to point out at this juncture that these first two levels of relatedness potentials—*Organizing* and *Symbiotic* arise in the earliest months and years of life before verbal symbolism and narrational skills develop and therefore are not rememberable in words or stories, but rather in body sensations and emotional-interactional habits. This fact has crucial implications for suicide interventions. That is, if it is true, as I am contending, that intentional suicides and instrumental gestures and attempted suicides all have their unconscious origins in these earliest developmental epochs, then it follows that there are no words or stories to express the re-enactments of primordial traumatic experiences. Therefore, answers to questions as to the why and wherefore of an individual's suicidal behaviors simply cannot be answered—cannot be put into words or stories. Rather, people tend to point to triggering events or to make up reasons that appear to hold water but in fact fail to represent the deep mind-body anguish involved. The bottom line: *people cannot tell us why they attempted or gestured or succeeded in the suicidal impulse.* Speech and stories only become coherent by the third year of life and memories and reports representing those later experiences are more reliable though various forms of unconsciousness are always at play. But since traumas of the organizing and symbiotic era hold the key to understanding suicidality there is no way for suicidal people to tell us what their deep unconscious experience and needs are at the moment. Instead the memories that are being enacted are marked with the body/mind agony of Psycheache.

In the third-year *Self-other experience,* the self-relatedness mode feeds off of the praise and admiration of others to bolster an otherwise weak or not yet stabilized sense of self. The transfer to therapy is a re-enactment of the need for affirmation or twinning from the therapist-other. It's not that suicide might not become accidentally triggered by events, but so long as one is feeling adequately affirmed in life suicide is not an option. My favorite example is Gustav Flaubert's *Madam Bovary* who uses everyone and everything to bolster her fragile self-esteem—until she is at last publicly exposed in her adulterous treachery and fragments into cyanide— the call of darkness with relief from her mad self-aggrandizing frenzy. Businessmen who have had a calamitous turn of fortune may leap from buildings or shoot themselves because their self-worth and pride has been based on what they were able to amass and control. However, often enough the grandiose self of the narcissist tends to ignore or move right past humiliation or injury. So it would seem that actual suicides resulting from *Self-other* failures of affirmation are relatively rare, impulsive, and desperate.

In the *Independent experience*, i.e., "normal"/"neurotic" relating, most everyone from time to time hits a deep discouragement or humiliating embarrassment and feels like "maybe it's time to throw in the towel" or "life just isn't worth it." But while the ideations may reflect a depressive moment, they are seldom long-lasting, manipulative, or instrumental and pass when the situation passes. We usually "can get by with a little help from our friends." In therapy the meaning of the discouragement or defeat is free associated to until it dissipates or the conflict is resolved.

High-risk behaviors may be frequent with some people at either of these two more complex levels of relatedness experience.

When and if the person is ready to examine them they will likely be revealed to be related to some self-esteem issues (*Self-other*) or some triangular (*Independent*) relatedness conflict.

Before you read further be sure you have firmly in mind the ways each level of relatedness experience transfers into later in life relationships and later in life interpersonal situations so that the illustrations that follow will be clear. That is, in considering completed and attempted suicides our interest will be mainly in the first two pre-verbal kinds of infantile trauma that may appear in adult life when triggered by some relational situation. We will follow these themes through film as well as literary and case illustrations.

To Review:

- **Organizing transfer** is some kind of avoidance or rupture of connectedness or competence in order to avoid anticipated traumatizing over- or under-stimulating relational situations.

- **Symbiotic transfer** is behavior (unconsciously) designed to be instrumental in getting one's early relatedness needs met according to a certain restrictive but familiar pattern or style.

- **Self-other transfer** represents enactments aimed to get responses from the other to bolster self-esteem.

- **Independent transfer** is a re-enactment of competitive and cooperative triangular conflicts from childhood in current relational settings.

Aside on the Universality of Relational Traumas

It is understood that we all participate in all of these relatedness modes, transferring them into our relationships on a daily basis. But because of excessive under- or over-stimulating trauma in the development of any of these early modes we may emphasize one relatedness style or another on a chronic or periodic basis. It is my contention that suicides as well as gestures and attempts invariably tap into some early preverbal trauma in such a way that unbearable mind-body anguish is experienced. We may then recall emotionally similar experiences that happened in later development and can be recalled in pictures, words and stories—thus "telescoping" the impact of early body-mind trauma through more rememberable experiences into the present triggering interpersonal situation. Said differently, early impactful interpersonal trauma that can only be remembered in somatic and emotional interactional experience may come to be represented by a later memory of similar emotional impact, so that several memories become linked together that finally point to the origin of relational trauma in infancy.

Chapter Two
Why the Call to "Darkness"?

There is a simple answer to this question and a more complex theoretical one. But in either case, to those vulnerable to occasional or frequent bouts of depression and suicidality, the call of darkness is no mere metaphor but a compelling and terrifying reality.

The simple answer rests on early life experiences—the rhythm of waking and sleeping activity of a fetus and neonate and the earliest emergence of consciousness out of non-consciousness. In waking activity both before and after birth the earliest sense of agency is deployed into encounters with sustained sensorimotor experiences of otherness that alternate with lapses into sleep—darkness. By the fourth month the forays into otherness experience take on a definite intentional seeking quality involving expectation so that the processes of developing human consciousness and mutual affect regulation truly get off the ground. Thus, during the third trimester and during what infant researchers are now calling the fourth trimester, the infant is *organizing* channels of connection to her world—both physical and mental until moments of anticipatory and sustained seeking reliably begin.

The pediatrician-psychoanalyst Donald Winnicott speaks of the baby's "going on being" in the first three months and the importance of the mother's "total maternal preoccupation" during this time so that the organizing efforts are reinforced in a timely manner and are not thwarted by unnecessary intrusions or delays—so that the infant is not forced to begin "thinking", that is, trying to figure things out before she is ready.

But we know that many things can and do go wrong to impinge on these early organizing activities—premature birth, adoption at birth, incubators, surgeries, illnesses, depressed or crazy mothers, raging and alcoholic fathers, marital strife, environmental stresses, hostile siblings, invasive toxins, neglectful or abusive caregivers, pets, or even rats in the crib. Impingements disrupt baby's reaching forays midstream in baby's deployment of her perceptual-motor explorations resulting in under- or over-stimulating experiences and the "never reach that way again" becomes established.

Babies vigorously protest intrusions into their need space and may kick, scream, cry, arch their backs, hold their breaths, bang their heads or flail wildly in pain and angst until exhausted and then fall into sleep—the peaceful retreat of "darkness", the relief of unconsciousness. Vulnerable individuals later in life may have this early retreat to peace and darkness triggered in situations of extreme hopelessness, helplessness, despair and psychic pain. Or, conversely and paradoxically, in otherwise positive situations that are anticipated to bring successful connection with another. That is, *the anticipation of an otherwise satisfying interpersonal (or social) situation may trigger retreat or collapse into the relief of darkness because in infancy the original reaching experience resulted in a traumatic disaster.*

The more complex answer to the question "Why darkness?" relates to an issue Sigmund Freud worked over during his entire professional career from his earliest papers in the 1890s to his final papers in the late 1930s, a phenomenon he referred to as "the splitting of the ego."[11] By this Freud meant that the earliest sense of agency, "the I", necessarily becomes split as it deals with the world. That is, while one part of "the I" reaches explorationally into the world, another part of "the I" maps what it finds—that is, *actively creates and in some sense then becomes an internal representation* of what is out there.

In the illuminating 1943 paper "Identification", Hungarian psychoanalyst Alice Balint expands Freud's thinking on the ego, "the I," creating a perceptual-motor-affect identity inside that mirrors an object-affect identity on the outside—through the process of "identification."[12] One might say there is a "me-self" and an "other-self" both in the ego, "the I." Psychoanalyst Otto Kernberg speaks of the building blocks of personality being comprised of "a representation of self, a representation of other, and an affect linking them—so that there is always a "split I" but in ordinary development the split becomes smoothly integrated into a developmental building block.[13] But when in infancy the "other-self" is experienced as traumatizing then the interactional-narrational quality of the internalized other is likewise traumatizing. That is, the sequence and affect quality of the perceptual-motor reaching out to contact "otherness" comes to take on a negative or traumatizing *internalized* narrational quality.

In the *Organizing* experience the internalized narrational quality requires a shutdown, a retreat toward or into darkness—a

---

[11] S. Freud (1938).
[12] Balint (1943).
[13] Kernberg (1975).

loss of consciousness. In the *Symbiotic* experience the internalized narrational quality is that of creating compelling mutual affect regulation or interactional scenarios. That is, the unique mother-child symbiotic (attachment or mutual affect regulation) scenarios are of an *instrumental* nature—each person behaves in a way designed to get her needs in the relationship met. These internalized instrumental scenarios reappear in later life as (usually unconscious) interactional efforts to compel the other to meet my psychological needs according to my internalized expectations. Said differently, when the *Organizing* experience is re-activated in later life there is psychic pain and the call of darkness. When the *Symbiotic* experience is activated in later life there is anxiety and pressure to get the other to "do it my way." It seems then that completed suicides are most likely derived from *Organizing* experience while various kinds of suicide attempts and gestures are more likely derived from the internalized instrumental scenarios of the *Symbiotic* experience.

But however one chooses to think of this basic process of creating or internalizing a subjective world based on the ways one *experiences* the external objective world, in the earliest months of life the early external world may offer some hard knocks. For example, French psychoanalyst Andre Green speaks of the "dead mother" as an internal under-stimulating representation of a blank-white, empty, dead but nevertheless present early maternal environment that colors one's subsequent experiences of emptiness in the world.[14] Conversely, *when a child is forced by traumatic over-stimulation to retreat into the peace and darkness of*

---

[14] Green (1986).

unconsciousness and sleep, blackness and darkness is internalized as a refuge against reaching in some way that has intolerably and painfully failed. In later life idiosyncratic forms of interpersonal or social reaching in anticipation of success and fulfillment may paradoxically trigger the other side of the split ego into experiencing either white, blank emptiness or a painful collapse into darkness.

Suicidologist Edwin Shneidman considers the relation between our cultural attitudes toward sleep and suicide. He asks: "Are there, for certain individuals, some instructive parallels between overt self-destructive behaviors and changes in ordinary states of consciousness, especially sleep?...The kinship between death and sleep is in our folk language. There are at least four kinds of relationships that can be distinguished. (1) Sleep is seen as the replenisher of life. (2) Sleep is also seen as "unplugging" from life. (3) Sleep is called the brother of death. (4) Sleep is substituted for suicide."[15]

We are altogether too familiar with great and famous personages, creative writers, and artists who at the peak of their creative careers with anticipation of increased future personal and interpersonal successes choose the call of darkness and suicide. Those who have later written about their experience invariably speak of the anguish of unbearable physical and mental pain having been there in various ways for a lifetime and that with near success experiences in external life the terrifying internal anticipatory pain becomes unbearable—the split "crushing-other" side of the infant ego wins out. People who have experienced suicide attempts and later succeeded have written extensively on

---

[15] Shneidman (2014).

41

the compulsion, the drive, the addictive imperative of responding to the call of darkness.[16] Later we will look at how some of these highly successful and creative people have characterized the call of darkness.

On the other hand, suicide *attempters* and *ideationists* may have depressive temperaments or depressive moments but lack this internalized compulsion to seek the peace and rest of endless Darkness. An illustration from film at this point may help put meaning into these difficult theoretical considerations.

@The Suicide Room

The remarkable Polish film *@The Suicide Room* illustrates exactly the suicide dynamics just outlined. It was written and directed by Jan Komasa and released in 2011—winning numerous international awards for the Best Actor (Jakub Gierszal), Best Actress, Best Screenplay, and Best Film.

18-year-old Dominik is a sensitive and lost teenager. This son of wealthy success-driven parents is about to graduate from high

---

[16] The following books give telling personal accounts of suicide survivors:

Alvarez, A. (1971). *The Savage God: A Study of Suicide.* Harmondsworth, UK: Penguin.

Blauner, S.R. (2002). *How I Stayed Alive When My Brain Was Trying to Kill Me: One Person's Guide to Suicide Prevention.* New York: HarperCollins.

Jamison, K.R. (1999). *Night Falls Fast: Understanding Suicide.* New York: Alfred A. Knopf.

Miller, J. (ed.) (1992). *On Suicide: Great writers on the ultimate question.* San Francisco: Chronicle Books.

Styron, W. (1992). *Darkness Visible.* London: Picador.

Webb, D. (2013*). Thinking about Suicide.* Reprint edition. Ross-on-Wye, U.K.:PCCS.

Wise, T. L. (2003). *Waking Up: Climbing Through the Darkness.* Los Angeles: Pathfinder.

school with highest honors. He now must study diligently for his final exams in order to ensure his admittance to the prestigious university for which his parents have groomed him for a lifetime.

The film opens at a concert where Dominik and his parents listen to Schubert's lied *"Der doppelgänger"* (The Double), a sad song about lost love and the grieving shadow of darkness.

Der doppelgänger

The night is quiet, the streets are calm,
In this house my beloved once lived:
She has long since left the town,
But the house still stands, here in the same place.

A man stands there also and looks to the sky,
And wrings his hands, overwhelmed by pain:
I am terrified – when I see his face,
The moon shows me my own form!

O you Doppelgänger! you pale comrade!
Why do you ape the pain of my love
Which tormented me upon this spot
So many a night, so long ago?

–text by Heinrich Hein (1928)

Dominik, avoiding studying for his exams, soon becomes fascinated with a self-harm video he has found on the Internet. He responds to a post that takes him to the Suicide Room where he begins chatting with people who want to kill themselves.

While drinking at an after-prom party when a girl admits to some lesbian experimentation she agrees to demonstrate girl-kissing to her friends if Dominik will kiss Alexander (with whom everyone knows Dominik is desperately and hopelessly in love). The kiss turns out to be long and passionate. Dominik suffers considerable teasing afterward as a result.

Later during judo practice with Alexander they wrestle and while Alexander has him pinned to the floor humping him Dominik spontaneously ejaculates leading to further embarrassment, teasing and some violent bullying from classmates.

With a slightly blackened eye Dominik goes to the Suicide Room. Each person in the chat room has an avatar. He encounters the red-haired Silvia and chooses to show his face to her. When she shows her face she has on a partial mask. When he asks her about the mask she says, "it protects me from harmful people and substances." She has not left her room in her parents' home for three years. She desperately wants to kill herself.

Dominik asks, "Do you need help? Maybe you would like me to call someone? Get someone to see you?"

She: "Look, look! Take a good look!" She raises her cut and bleeding arm: "I'll fucking cut myself, I will! Razors are my friend. They have very sharp tongues."

He: "Why do you want to kill yourself?"

She: "Why don't you want to kill yourself?"

He: "To live."

She: "And I want to kill myself to die. I need to pluck up the courage and I'll do it."

The people in the Suicide Room discuss how they want to kill themselves. Silvia begs Dominik to get her some pills from his psychiatrist to give to her. She instructs him what pills to get and how many and names a bar where she will meet him at midnight to get the pills. He feigns insomnia and desperation in order to get

44

some sleep so he can study for his exams and obtains the requested pills from his doctor.

His addiction to the Internet has infuriated his parents because he is refusing to study for the all-important senior final exams that will determine if he can attend the university his parents have chosen for him. He barricades himself in his room on the Internet refusing to study. [Note here that the success of graduating with high honors and the threat of being admitted to the most prestigious of universities immobilizes Dominik.]

In a rage his father rips out the Internet. Dominik pleads with mother to intervene but she is helpless in the face of father's abusive rage at the boy. His parents begin quarreling violently and this forces Dominik to come out of his room to protect his mother from his father's blows. They get him to talk about his experience in the Suicide Room. "You're there for them and they're there for you. They have helped me. They accepted me like a family, they must be worrying now that they can't reach me."

Mother: "These people are like a family?"

He: "Yes."

He wants to let his friends in the Suicide Room know he's OK but his father refuses. No Internet ever! Distraught that his Internet connection has been destroyed and he has lost contact with Silvia, he takes the promised pills and sneaks out to the bar. He waits patiently, drinking beer after beer getting woozy until an hour past midnight when he realizes that he has been stood up. He goes to the men's room with the intention of flushing the pills but finds himself downing them all himself. Coming out of the men's room starting into a drunken delirium he runs into a couple in the hallway making out, laughing and having fun and all three of them start playing together hugging and mutually videoing each other as he goes insanely wild finally crashing to the floor. In his delirium fantasy while wallowing on the floor he returns to the barroom where the red-headed beauty Silvia is waiting for him in a smiling and seductive aura of romantic mystery. In fantasy Dominik reaches for the kind of loving, fulfilling and mystical connection he has longed for since infancy.

But his doppelgänger, his shadow of darkness, has at last caught up with him. Dominik, wildly flailing on the floor screaming for Mother to come rescue him, finally collapses as the curtain of endless Darkness drops.

We see here the key ingredients for the *Organizing Experience* suicide. The filmmaker opens with the Doppelgänger, the split self, the shadow of sadness and ancient thwarted love that remains to torture him. We then have the helpless mother who is violently prevented by father from rescuing the boy from his anguish and rage. In his isolated distress—a re-enactment from infancy?—Dominik is at the peak of his academic success on the verge of admission to an idealized life of wealth and happiness when he suddenly retreats into the Suicide Room with the fantasy of regaining his lost love of infancy, the call of darkness. His final screams are, "Mother, *Mother!*"

Were his frustrated homosexuality and bullying the trigger? Was his father's violence and his mother's helplessness the trigger? Was his discovering suicidal friends in the chat room the trigger? Was being stood up by Silvia the trigger? We can't be sure. But the filmmaker makes clear that Dominik had an appointment with his Doppelgänger, the shadow of his mystical lost love of infancy that issued *the call of sarkness.*

The Epicenter, "Psycheache"

It was the universally acclaimed world expert on suicidality, Edwin Schneidman, who died in 2009 at the age of 91, who coined the word and the study, "suicidology." In the late 1950s Schneidman while doing some doctoral research inadvertently discovered and later retrieved a large number of suicide notes from the Los Angeles coroner's office that he and his colleagues subjected to careful scientific scrutiny in the hopes of discovering what makes people who succeed in suicide different from those who attempt suicide and normal controls who were asked to simulate suicide notes according to their imagination. The results were overall disappointing but the research team established an evidence-based approach to the study of suicide. He founded in 1962 the Los Angeles Suicide Prevention Center (along with Norman Farberow and Robert Litman)—the first of its kind, and then went on to organize other suicide prevention centers and societies on national and international levels as well as to begin a journal of suicidology. Shneidman conducted countless "suicide autopsies" which were after-the-fact attempts to amass any and all data and findings from all possible sources and to systematically study it to see what cause or causes could be discerned. We will later review one of these very impressive and revealing autopsies.

After an illustrious career with many books and countless articles and reviews Schneidman came to believe a number of things.

1. First, he saw suicide as uncompromisingly an act of the human *mind*—not of biology, physiology, or sociology—

though the mental pain was also physical.

2. Then, after watching endless researchers try to define suicide in diverse ways and do frequency counts according to a host of variables in a variety of settings throughout the world without decisive results, Shneidman concluded that each and every suicide gesture, threat, attempt, or success was absolutely unique and that *only the intense study of the individual case would yield enlightening results.*

3. Most importantly for our purposes here, Shneidman clearly located the suicidal dynamic in earliest developmental experience—but he believed that during his lifetime there was not yet enough infant research data to define what those early experiences might be or to theorize extensively about what factors in early development laid the seeds for later suicidality. This emphasis on needing a viable theory of relational development to explain the suicidal impulse on the basis of very early life experiences is echoed by many voices throughout the suicide literature. The present book proposes a viable Relational Listening theory that addresses the kinds of infant experiences that constitute the sources of different kinds of suicidality.

Late in his career Shneidman coined the word "Psycheache" to designate the subjective center of each person's pain. That is, suicidal clients usually have many stories to tell, many reasons for considering suicide, and many background factors that can be discussed endlessly and fruitlessly. But Shneidman's relentless question became, "Where do you hurt?" "How can I help you?" These are now bywords of suicide workers everywhere because if asked persistently these questions will inevitably lead to the epicenter of the individual's suicidal urge. Some results from this questioning the pain approach occur almost immediately and other results develop slowly over time.

As a follow-up, in his book *The Suicidal Mind*, Schneidman says, "I have proposed the view that suicide is prevented by changing our perception of the situation, and by redefining what is unbearable. Perceiving that there are other possible ways of seeing things—redefining the impossible, bearing the unbearable, swallowing the indigestible bolus of shame or guilt."[17]

The Relational Listening approach to suicide intervention being presented here was first developed in the study of early developmental experiences as they became enacted and expressed in the course of psychoanalytic psychotherapy that was essentially unrelated to the question of suicide. The Relational Listening approach to the study of early infant and child development is based on emerging infant research and puts forth a theory about the kinds of relational experiences that can plant the seeds for later suicide, suicide attempts, and suicidal ideation—a theory that Shneidman and many others have long been calling for. Further, in understanding the source of the pain in pre-verbal, pre-symbolic internalized experiences of early infant care and trauma, there are definite directions that orient useful forms of psychotherapy—in short, finding ways to represent in here-and-now relational consciousness the otherwise unrepresentable terrors of one's psycheache.

On the basis of our understanding of early relational

---

[17] Shneidman (1998).

development we might say that the experiential seeds to later suicidality are deeply personal and idiosyncratic, bound up as they are in early relational experience. Early memories are carried in somatic experiences, affect regulation expectations, and interpersonal interaction scenarios—all of which precede and are dissociated from more developmentally complex forms of memory and consciousness. These early developmental memories can become known only through interpersonal enactments—the kind that are fostered by relational psychotherapy—as Freud said, by being repeated instead of being remembered.

We have all been living and enacting early preverbal and pre-symbolic relatedness modes for a lifetime in our daily relationships, especially our more emotionally significant ones. In more fortuitous moments with intimate relationship partners we may stumble upon a *Eureka!*—a moment of realization when the meaning of some often repeated piece of ourselves suddenly becomes clarified in consciousness. In relational forms of psychotherapy our entire endeavor is aimed at developing such *Eureka* experiences based on their transfer of life themes into the here-and-now of the therapeutic relationship. If we are searching for clues to our suicidality, an interpersonal enactment is invited that, when it occurs, allows the veil of mystery to be lifted so that we come to understand, for example, who it is we would really like to kill, or who we need to impel to meet our needs or whatever deeply personal issues may be a stake.

Psychotherapy experience makes clear that these primitive modes of relating that we enact daily can be framed in a therapeutic relationship designed to question at all times "what's going on here anyway?" Unfortunately, this is not a simple or quick task—it takes time to form an intimate, emotionally safe, authentic, and spontaneous relationship. The forms of therapy that are evolving to study the traumatic seeds of the past in the relational present inevitably require time and mutual dedication to the relationship process. Later I will survey some of the evolving forms of therapy that have emerged for the study of suicidality. For the time being let it be said that the promising forms of therapy (1) all center on a *mind* process that asks about the Psycheache, "Where does it hurt?" And (2) that they all expect the emerging fruitful insights to arrive in here-and-now enacted relationship experiences.

Three last points on relational memories:

1. First due to the splitting of the ego and the identification with traumatizing otherness, half of our ego takes on the role of the primitive intruding and hurtful other so that in relationships at times we may be doing to others (like our partner, our children, or our therapist) what was once done unto us! That is, we transfer into relational situations not only our exploratory me-self of infancy but also our identificatory traumatizing other-self and we may alternatingly or in tandem enact either or both roles. We can speak meaningfully of a passive-active "role reversal" of our me-self and our other-self.

2. Secondly, since memories from the *Organizing* and *Symbiotic* levels of relatedness in all of us exist in pre-symbolic and pre-narrational forms, we have no memorable images, pictures, stories or scenarios with which to represent those early relational experiences. But, as became manifestly clear in the "recovered memory"

movement of the 1990s, the dreaming, imagining mind is quite capable of constructing vivid pictures and stories that represent—in culturally-determined archetypal metaphors—the otherwise unrememberable and unrepresentable traumatic memories of early relationships that have been preserved in somatic and interactional modes. The most common archetypal metaphors that were used to "remember" otherwise unrememberable and traumatic experiences were alien abduction, satanic ritual abuse, childhood incest, rape, abuse, dismemberment and other unspeakable experiences. The mistake was to take such archetypal memories literally rather than metaphorically and also not to attend to the interpersonal situation in which the intent was to create an *Organizing level breach of connection* or a *Symbiotic level instrumental demand* for literal belief from the therapist. In brief, the consensus of experts in the field is that the origin of suicidal impulses is in early life. The Relational Listening theoretical structure places these relational traumas in the first two years of life that are essentially pre-symbolic and preverbal. This means that all of the stories that are constructed to "explain" the whys and wherefores of suicide are culturally-determined archetypal narratives that people use to "explain" the otherwise unrememberable, inexplicable and/or unspeakable early events that are being triggered by relational situations in the present—almost always relating, of course, to loss of one type or another. The most common of these explanations are lost love, career failure, social isolation, illness, aging and other distressing life events. William Styron states that the anguish and physical pain of suicidality is "indescribable" so that those who have not experienced the extremes of regressive depression have no way to understand what the pain is like because there is nothing like it in normal ordinarily representable experience.[18]

3. Thirdly, as mentioned earlier, emotional memories "telescope" backwards—like a collapsible telescope. That is, some painful or shameful experience emblazoned on memory from high school or third grade reading circle may in fact be carrying the emotional charge from a traumatic experience actually originating in the first months and years of life. To illustrate, we each have numerous examples of something disturbing or frightening happening in a group setting (a family death or an earthquake) where one or two or several react "out of proportion" to the event as perceived by and reacted to by others. Those with intense and prolonged reactions have likely brought a telescoped memory from infancy experience into the event of the present that accounts for their exaggerated panic, rage, or mute response.

As examples of extraordinarily intelligent and creative people who on the verge of major success and acclaim heeded the call of darkness let us consider the subjective accounts of Sylvia Plath and William Styron.

---

[18] Styron (1990).

Sylvia Plath

I have what I believe is an example of telescoped memory, Sylvia Plath's remarkable poem "Daddy", written shortly before she killed herself at age 30. I am convinced that the poem in all its intense blackness and sadistic evil is representing some primal experience of a failed mothering process that left her utterly helpless, hopeless and in blackness, the call of darkness. Harriet Rosenstein in her critical biography of Plath provides enough information about her early history for me to feel that my interpretation is essentially correct.[19] It is common in therapy experience that when traumas are remembered about Daddy or other close personages of childhood or even later life, the powerful sting of emotion echoes a traumatic telescoped theme of infant relational development. This same telescoping phenomenon is characteristic of other forms of PTSD like major accidents or war experiences. One only gets a certain sense of corroboration through the hermeneutic process of repeated thematic similarities that occurs in life or psychotherapy.

Sylvia was born in 1932, at the height of the Great Depression. Her German-born father, Otto Plath, was professor of zoology and German at Boston University. Her mother, Aurelia Schober Plath, was 20 years his junior and a teacher of shorthand and typing. Aurelia gave birth to her brother when Sylvia was barely two years old so we have several factors that may have made her early years difficult enough so that Rosenstein and later Marris[20] speak of early trauma. Shortly after Sylvia's eighth birthday her father

---

[19] Rosenstein (1972).
[20] Maris (1981).

died of complications in a case of diabetes. She published her first poem shortly thereafter at age 8 in the *Boston Herald*. She was always an outstanding student receiving scholarships to Smith College and a Fulbright Fellowship to Cambridge. She married the English poet Ted Hughes. Sylvia experienced a miscarriage and then gave birth to two children before her marriage ran into trouble with her husband taking on a series of mistresses. She wrote the poem "Daddy" at the time they were divorcing. Shortly thereafter she killed herself by putting her head in a gas oven. My surmise is that the cruel abandonment of her husband echoed the traumatic loss of her father and that these experiences telescoped with early failures of maternal care.

We know that Plath suffered her whole life with intractable depression and had made several prior suicide attempts. We know that her father died when she was eight. We also know that at the peak of her successes like many other great artists, she killed herself at age 30 in 1963. Plath, prior to her suicide described her experience of depression: "I have been and am battling depression," she wrote in her journal. "I am now flooded with despair, almost hysteria, as if I were smothering. As if a great muscular owl were sitting on my chest, its talons clenching and constricting my heart."[21] And on the subject of the fear of great achievement, in her widely acclaimed autobiographical novel, *The Bell Jar*, her main character at one point ruminates,

> What I always thought I had in mind was getting some big scholarship to graduate school or a grant to study all over Europe, and then I thought I'd be a professor and

---

[21] Quoted in Jamison (2011).

write books of poems or write books and be an editor of some sort. Usually I had these plans on the tip of my tongue. 'I don't really know,' I heard myself say. I felt a deep shock, hearing myself say that, because the minute I said it, I knew it was true. It sounded true, and I recognized it....[22]

That is, the autobiographical character always believed she could strive for and attain greatness but with a quick slip revealed to herself the conviction that such success would or could never be achieved. Maris, in his review of Plath's life and work, states:

> Sylvia's early trauma led to a very basic and tenacious subjective inadequacy. All of her achievements, straight-A grades, prizes, fellowships, and awards could not substitute for her loss of early love and noncontingent approval. Respect and love are very different emotions. 'Mother love' is freely given, or withheld, without regard to merit; and later achievements, no matter how grand, can never substitute for early noncontingent acceptance....
>
> This inability to accept self and others led almost inexorably to social isolation. Plath became intensely, even painfully, critical, compulsive, perfectionistic, and rigid....[23]

The Bell Jar gives a vivid metaphor for Plath's experience of her life predicaments:

> I saw my life branching out before me like the green fig tree in the story. From the tip of every branch, like a fat purple fig, a wonderful future beckoned and winked. One fig was a husband and a happy home and children, and another fig was a famous poet and another fig was a brilliant professor, and another fig was Ee Gee, the

---

[22] Plath (2013).
[23] Maris, op. cit.

amazing editor, and another fig was Europe and Africa and South America, and another fig was Constantine and Socrates and Attila and a pack of other lovers with queer names and offbeat professions, and another fig was an Olympic lady crew champion, and beyond and above these figs were many more figs I couldn't quite make out.

I saw myself sitting in the crotch of this fig tree, starving to death, just because I couldn't make up my mind which of the figs I would choose. I wanted each and every one of them, but choosing one meant losing all the rest, and, as I sat there, unable to decide, the figs began to wrinkle and go black, and one by one, they plopped to the ground at my feet.[24]

Maris speaks further to Plath's life plight:

Plath's early trauma, rigidity, isolation, and lack of positive human interaction (of which sexual problems were just one facet) meant that her life had become unacceptable—not just unsatisfying, but intolerable. It was not long before the depression that had hounded her all her life turned irreversibly into hopelessness. As Plath herself wrote in The Bell Jar, "...my case was incurable."[25]

Rosenstein comes to essentially the same conclusion in her critical biography of Plath. Her last yet to be published poems were her best, she had reached a pinnacle of success as a poet:

Plath's late poetry is full of mouths, open, demanding, never satisfied. Those of children, of flowers, of animals, of other women, of men, and of her speakers. One's sense always is that the universe is insatiable because the speaker herself is insatiable. No amount of food, real or symbolic, can fill the emptiness within. And every demand from outside threatens to deplete her still

---

[24] Plath, op. cit.

[25] Maris, op. cit.

further, provocations thus to terror or rage. Her fate—
her dissolution—has in this and many other poems
["Daddy"] the ring of inevitability.[26]

In "Daddy" the speaker both needs her Daddy and needs to be free of her dependence on him. The need is that of a little child's need that has never been satisfied. The poem is a finalizing act of murder in which she severs herself from her compulsive internalized need to be neglected and abused. She sees herself as the archetypal victim—a Jewess being carried away in a cattle car but at the same time she feels erotically overwhelmed by his sadism. Her identification with his power to obliterate her leads her to attempt suicide earlier, but when that fails she resorts to other methods by turning him into a cruel black sadist that she is married to. In the end there is no escape, as she kills him, she kills herself.

The feminist movement of the 1960s and '70s, perhaps justifiably, seized onto this poem as a battle cry against male domination. But as a psychologist I read it as a representation of the otherwise un-representable primal mothering situation that was cruelly and seductively over-stimulating as well as overwhelming, depriving, and full of cruel blackness.

Daddy[27]

You do not do, you do not do
Any more, black shoe
In which I have lived like a foot
For thirty years, poor and white,
Barely daring to breathe or Achoo.

---

[26] Rosenstein (quoted in Maris), p. 131).
[27] Plath (2003).

Daddy, I have had to kill you.
You died before I had time —
Marble-heavy, a bag full of God,
Ghastly statue with one gray toe
Big as a Frisco seal

And a head in the freakish Atlantic
Where it pours bean green over blue
In the waters off beautiful Nauset.
I used to pray to recover you.
Ach, du.

In the German tongue, in the Polish town
Scraped flat by the roller
Of wars, wars, wars.
But the name of the town is common.
My Polack friend

Says there are a dozen or two.
So I never could tell where you
Put your foot, your root,
I never could talk to you.
The tongue stuck in my jaw.

It stuck in a barb wire snare.
Ich, ich, ich, ich,
I could hardly speak.
I thought every German was you.
And the language obscene

An engine, an engine
Chuffing me off like a Jew.
A Jew to Dachau, Auschwitz, Belsen.
I began to talk like a Jew.
I think I may well be a Jew.

The snows of the Tyrol, the clear beer of Vienna
Are not very pure or true.
With my gipsy ancestress and my weird luck
And my Taroc pack and my Taroc pack
I may be a bit of a Jew.

I have always been scared of you,
With your Luftwaffe, your gobbledygoo.
And your neat mustache
And your Aryan eye, bright blue.
Panzer-man, panzer-man, O You —

Not God but a swastika
So black no sky could squeak through.
Every woman adores a Fascist,
The boot in the face, the brute
Brute heart of a brute like you.

You stand at the blackboard, daddy,
In the picture I have of you,
A cleft in your chin instead of your foot
But no less a devil for that, no not
Any less the black man who

Bit my pretty red heart in two.
I was ten when they buried you.
At twenty I tried to die
And get back, back, back to you.
I thought even the bones would do.

But they pulled me out of the sack,
And they stuck me together with glue.
And then I knew what to do.
I made a model of you,
A man in black with a Meinkampf look

And a love of the rack and the screw.
And I said I do, I do.
So daddy, I'm finally through.
The black telephone's off at the root,
The voices just can't worm through.

If I've killed one man, I've killed two—
The vampire who said he was you
And drank my blood for a year,
Seven years, if you want to know.
Daddy, you can lie back now.

There's a stake in your fat black heart
And the villagers never liked you.
They are dancing and stamping on you.
They always knew it was you.
Daddy, daddy, you bastard, I'm through.

William Styron

Like Plath, for a lifetime William Styron, the much-celebrated author of *The Confessions of Nat Turner* (1967) and *Sophie's Choice* (1979), experienced moderate but intractable depression that he medicated with heavy alcohol usage and which he writes about in his 1990 *Darkness Visible: Memoir of Madness*. Styron is committed to considering Major Depression as a disease as serious as Diabetes or Cancer and that early childhood losses are critically influential.

Shortly after Styron had turned 60 early in the summer of 1985, he became unable physically to use his life-long medication for depression, alcohol, because of recurrent nausea. As the months went by, he found his life increasingly colorless and he became alternately seriously depressed and anxious, physically lethargic and finally totally unable to write.

During this same time period he had accepted an invitation to go to Paris in October to accept the prestigious and much coveted *Prix Mondial Cino del Duca* award in recognition of his extraordinary literary "humanism." He had received many awards and honors throughout his life and now he was reaching a peak in his illustrious career. Shortly prior to the trip his depression plummeted downward until he felt forced to make an appointment with a psychiatrist for when he returned to New

York in four days. He then describes a series of nightmarish depressive experiences in Paris of unendurable anguish and pain surrounding the honor being bestowed upon him. He describes his experience:

> I was feeling in my mind a sensation close to, but indescribably different from, actual pain. This leads me to touch again on the elusive nature of such distress. It has to be emphasized that if the pain were readily describable most of the countless sufferers from this ancient affliction would have been able to confidently depict for their friends and loved ones (even their physicians) some of the actual dimensions of their torment, and perhaps elicit a comprehension that has been generally lacking; such incomprehension has usually been due not to a failure of sympathy but to the basic inability of healthy people to imagine a form of torment so alien to everyday experience.[28]

Back in New York with medications and psychotherapy his depression softened but continued to spiral downward. He writes:

> Depression is a disorder of mood, so mysteriously painful and elusive in the way it becomes known to the self—to the mediating intellect—as to verge close to being beyond description. It thus remains nearly incomprehensible to those who have not experienced it in its extreme mode, although the gloom, "the blues" which people go through occasionally and associate with the general hassle of everyday existence are of such prevalence that they do give many individuals a hint of the illness in its catastrophic form. But at the time of which I write I had descended far past those familiar, manageable doldrums. In Paris, I am able to see now, I was at a critical stage in the development of the disease

---

[28] Styron (1990), p. 19.

situated at an ominous way station between its unfocused stirrings earlier that summer and the near violent denouement of December, which sent me into the hospital.[29]

He describes the sense of resoluteness about finding a way to end the pain. He reports experiencing "a wraithlike observer who, not sharing the dementia of his double," his doppelganger, watched with dispassionate curiosity as his companion was struggling with the oncoming disaster. He begins settling his various businesses, rewriting his will, and determining the ways at hand to end it all. Then, on the final night, he destroyed the personal notebook that he had kept for years, and after his wife had gone upstairs to bed, he put on a movie to while away some time before she went to sleep. In the movie characters were milling about outside of a music conservatory and from the distance came a contralto voice and the soaring passage from Brahms's *Alto Rhapsody*—which put him immediately in touch with the joys of his childhood and his family life and before he could kill himself he woke his wife to take him to the hospital. He was hospitalized seven weeks and in therapy and recovery for several years before he was able to write about his experiences. "In the hospital I partook of what may be depression's only grudging favor—its ultimate capitulation." Styron came to believe that his childhood with a severely depressed father and a mother unavailable from infancy who died when he was thirteen, left him with "incomplete mourning" which he finally completed in therapy. *Darkness Visible* is full of experiences of an entire lifetime that certainly constitute the call of darkness.

---

[29] *Ibid.*, p. 6.

I hope my theoretical perspectives and these two illustrations make clear why peaceful, painless "Darkness"—loss of consciousness—is sought by those who have experienced severe infantile shut-down traumas. In a later chapter we will return to more accounts of people on the brink of success fleeing anticipated re-traumatization by heeding the call of darkness.

In this book I am most concerned with the *Organizing* experience since it is my belief that the majority of *seriously intended completed suicides* stem from internalized traumatic relatedness shut-down templates originating in the earliest months of life—although there are completed suicides that might have been only attempts except for either impulsiveness or an accident. Further, I believe that *most attempted suicides and suicidal gestures* stem from internalized relational templates originating in the *Symbiotic* experience that are primarily instrumental—that is, are desperate attempts to get the world or others in the world to aid in meeting my emotional and psychological needs and relieving my internalized abandonment pains. And there are situations in which previous instrumental attempts become converted into full intentional suicide. In either case Shneidman's crucial questions, "Where does it hurt?" and "How can I help you?" remain central to any therapeutic approach.

I would now like to illustrate the instrumental type of suicide attempt that finally changes into suicide in the film *Fatal Attraction*. Perhaps you never thought of it as a film about suicide!

Fatal Attraction

You all know the 1987 film written by James Deardon–but you don't know the real ending because the studio audiences vetoed it in favor of a cowboy-and-Indian style dramatic ending where the wicked witch is shot dead. But *Fatal Attraction* was written and originally produced as a suicide movie.

There is the apparently chance meeting at a bar between Dan (Michael Douglas) and Alex (Glenn Close) during a business cocktail party, followed by coffee and mad passionate sex. Careful scrutiny of the opening scene, however, reveals that Alex spots her prey and positions herself carefully by the drink ordering station so she could lure him in. The following morning she pursues him and during her seduction luncheon we hear the final suicide scene from *Madame Butterfly* playing in the background. Dan firmly reminds her again that he is married with a family and that their encounter was simply a chance meeting and that he must go back to his wife. Screaming, Alex accuses him of being selfish and self-centered, flies into a rage, and slashes her wrist.

In a "making of the movie" interview Glenn Close explained that as she tried to get into the mind of her character, she invented the business in the next scene that begins with her sitting by a lamp again listening to *Madam Butterfly.* She is turning the light off and then on and then off and then on as if she's grasping the split in her personality and that she feels her insanity and the suicidal call of darkness—all while Dan enjoys his family, his friends, and bowls happily with his buddies.

In the middle of the night sleeping next to his wife the phone rings and Alex demands that Dan meet her the next day. At the meeting she announces she is in love with him and over his protest she announces that she's pregnant—whereupon he offers to help her with an abortion but she is clear she *wants* his baby.

Driving home that night he finds a cassette tape on the seat of his car which he plays only to hear her declare again her love and her rage at him for being selfish and accusing him of being homosexual.

Then comes the scene we all recall in which his wife Beth (Anne Archer) comes into the house and sees a large pot boiling on the stove while her six-year-old child Ellen runs out to the rabbit hutch only to discover that her pet rabbit is missing.

Desiring to seduce the affections of the child, Alex kidnaps Ellen after school and takes her to Cony Island for a roller coaster ride. Meanwhile, mother Beth—while frantically searching for her kidnapped child—has a terrible automobile accident and ends up in the hospital.

In a rage Dan breaks into Alex's apartment and nearly strangles her while roughing her up on the floor with slaps and wild threats. Gasping for breath she manages to seize the kitchen knife and lunges at him. He wrests the knife from her and slowly backs out of her apartment making clear he was finished and carefully leaving the knife on the kitchen cabinet.

Next, in the ending you saw that was prepared for box office audiences, Beth is out of the hospital and upstairs examining her bruises in the bathroom mirror when behind her she sees Alex coming with a knife and a frantic struggle ensues. Dan downstairs in the kitchen responds quickly to the screams and finally pins Alex under the water in the bathtub until she goes limp. As he turns away exhausted from the fray, Alex springs from the bathtub knife in hand lunging at him when a shot is fired from the door by Beth and the audience cheers—at last the wicked witch is dead!

But the original and much more appropriate ending to the film is quite different. Mother, father, and child are raking leaves in the back yard of their suburban home when two squad cars pull up and father is introduced to two homicide inspectors. He admits being at Alex's apartment the night before and is then informed that she is dead. We watch horror spread across his face as he is arrested for suspected murder. He yells at his wife to go to his address book and get the number and call his attorney to meet him at the police station. While she is at the telephone she discovers in his address book the tape that had been in his car earlier and slides it into the recorder only to hear Alex in a desperate voice saying "I love you. And if I can't have you, I will have to kill myself."

The final scene in the original film is a flashback to the night before at Alex's apartment after Dan has left her for good. Hopelessly depressed Alex is propped up on the couch with the large knife in hand. We again hear on the stereo the concluding suicidal strains of *Madame Butterfly* as Alex slowly slits her throat— the call of darkness.

The box office ending changes entirely the interpretation of the film from the "fatal attraction" of Dan to a crazy woman to the "fatal attraction" of Alex to the one she must succeed at having or die.

One interesting side note is that in the original final scene Alex is seated Japanese style and slits her throat from the left side the way Japanese women typically commit suicide, not knife in the belly which is usually the way Madam Butterfly is played but is the way Japanese men typically commit suicide! The original version is elegant and true to the psychodynamics of the *Organizing*

Experience but was, as so often happens in Hollywood, traded in for an audience thrilling ending.

Chapter Three
Some General Considerations Regarding Suicide

Brief Historical Sketch

Here are a few highlights in the history of studies of suicide:

- In 1621, Robert Burton's *The Anatomy of Melancholy*[30] linked suicide to madness and argued for compassion for those who were so despairing as to kill themselves. Prior to that the law considered suicide criminal and the church a grave sin.

- In 1626 *Biathanatos*, John Donne declared in that suicide was under certain circumstances understandable and forgivable.

- In 1758's *Candide*, Voltaire described individuals who committed suicide as those "who voluntarily put an end to their misery."

- In 1765, Swiss philosopher Johann Bernhard Merian introduced the concept of suicide as illness, stating that suicide is not a criminal act but a mental illness.

- In 1838, Jean Esquirol, psychiatrist of the French Revolution, led the way in medicalizing insanity with his *Treatise on Insanity*.

---

[30] Burton (1621).

- In 1879's *Le Suicide*,[31] Emile Durkheim, the French father of modern sociology, sociologized suicide by explicating it in terms of society's tendency to integrate its members (or not), and to regulate the way they think, feel, and act. The more tightly organized the society or religion the fewer choices and the fewer suicides.

- In 1910, Sigmund Freud and his followers psychologized suicide in the meetings of the Vienna Psychoanalytical Society.[32]

- In his *Notebooks, 1914-1917*, Ludwig Wittgenstein wrote, "If suicide is allowed, then everything is allowed. If anything is not allowed, then suicide is not allowed."

- In 1917, Freud's "Mourning and Melancholia" focused on the unconscious turning of aggression against the self, an idea that galvanized psychological thinking for the next 40 years.[33]

- In 1930, M. Halbwach's in *The Causes of Suicide* sought to incorporate notions borrowed from Bergson within a Durkheimian framework; one of the consequences of this was that he stressed the importance of psychology in the explanation of social conduct much more than Durkheim tended to do.[34]

---

[31] Durkheim (1879).
[32] S. Freud (1910), 11:232.
[33] S. Freud (1917).
[34] Halbwachs (1930).

- In 1940, Albert Camus opens *The Myth of Sisyphus* with, "There is but one serious philosophic problem and that is suicide."

- In the early 1960s, Edwin Shneidman, Norman Farberow, Robert Litman, and others established the Los Angeles Suicide Prevention Center—the first of its kind—and began a deluge of studies that has continued into the present.

- In 1968, Shneidman took the lead in founding the American Association of Suicidology. The Association established a journal devoted to suicide and related subjects, *Suicide and Life-Threatening Behavior.*

- In 1983, John Birtchnell declares, "The more respectful the therapist is of the patient's right to take his own life, the more open will the patient be about his suicidal intent." He asserts that after a period of psychotherapy the patient's suicidal resolve should be respected when it is based on a clear appraisal that his situation is personally intolerable.[35]

- In 1987, The American Suicide Foundation was incorporated under the leadership of Dr. Herbert Hendin and now funds suicide research across the United States.

Well-Known People in History Who Have Committed Suicide:

- Petronius, opening and closing his veins at pleasure, exchanged gossip with his friends as he let out his blood for the last time.

---

[35] Birtchnell (1983) p. 473.

- Seneca and Socrates, having gone out of favor were their own executioners.

- Hero in the Hellespont, Sappho from the rock at Neritos, Cleopatra, Jocasta the mother and wife of Oedipus, Portia who would follow Brutus, and Paulina after Seneca all took their lives.

- In our time we could consider Hart Crane, Cesare Pavese, Virginia Woolf, Vargas, Plath, Hemingway, Bridgman (the Nobel laureate), and notable others like Robin Williams.

Classifications of Suicide

There have been literally thousands of suicide studies from around the world since the beginning of time resulting in various legal, religious, and moral restrictions set according to time, cultural orientations and location. But since the mid-nineteenth century scientific studies have sought:

- To classify various kinds of suicide as pathological, panic, altruistic, anomic, egotistic, passive, chronic, religious, or political;

- To correlate suicide with such things as atmospheric pressure, sunspots, and seasonal and economic fluctuations;

- To correlate suicide with many different biological and neurological conditions such as heredity, pregnancy, and menstruation;

- To study suicide in relation to tuberculosis, leprosy, alcoholism, syphilis, psychosis, diabetes;

- To study suicides in school, in the army, in prison, in corporations;

- To classify rates of suicide per hundred thousand by age, sex, religion, race, gender orientation, sexual preference, or region;

- To study attitudes towards suicide in different times and places; and

- To classify kinds and frequencies of suicide as they change in relation to different historical periods and cultural attitudes.

None of these many studies has arrived at a viable theory about the nature of suicide or come up with a reliable approach to assessment, treatment, and prevention

Collective Forms of Suicide:

- The heroic charge of a brigade,

- The ritual suicide of *suttee.*

- Those employed to die as a political assassins or *kamikaze* pilots,

- Hara-kiri or seppuku (belly-cutting) of Japanese men— for women throat-slitting,

- Tribe-protecting suicides among the Ardjiligjuar Eskimos (a rate sixty times greater than Canada as a whole), and other endangered groups; and

- Cult suicides like Jonestown.

Passionate Forms of Suicide:

- To get revenge against one's enemies,
- To give others anguish,
- To manipulate the world,
- To rage at frustration,
- To avoid humiliation over financial ruin,
- To avoid shame over public exposure,
- To expiate guilt,
- To avoid anxious terror,
- To assuage the melancholy of illness and ageing,
- To cure loneliness, abandonment, grief, apathy, emptiness,
- To express drunken despair and despair over failure, especially failure in love,
- To leap from the pinnacle of success,
- To avoid physical suffering from torture or disease, or imprisonment, or capture in war,
- To cry for help, and
- To cry in pain.

Psychotherapists' Commitment to Understanding Personal Meanings

But none of these categories of suicide help psychotherapists who are committed to helping people understand *personal meanings in their interpersonal life contexts*. A therapist assumes that each life and death are unique in meaning and that the *deep subjective meanings* of a person's suicidality—not necessarily the culturally appropriate narratives attached to it—are of the same importance as any other concern of the person who comes for therapeutic self-understanding.

What follows are a series of ideas taken from numerous sources designed to flesh out our understanding of how complex suicidality is.

Selected Suicide Statistics

Needless to say, there are endless statistics on all aspects of suicidality but I have selected a few representative statistics to insert at this point that give the overall flavor of the nature and trending direction of the worldwide epidemic.

- **The suicide rate of youths in the United States aged 15 to 24 has more than tripled since 1953**—the increase being largely in the male population.[36]

- **Suicide is the third leading cause of death for young people ages 12–18.**[37]

- In a typical 12-month period, nearly **14 percent of American high school students seriously consider suicide; nearly 11 percent make plans about how they would end their lives; and 6.3 percent actually attempt suicide.**[38]

- **32 percent of the nation's students ages 12–18 reported being bullied.** Of these students: 21 percent said they were bullied once or twice a month. 10 percent

---

[36] Crook., (2004), Kindle version, p. 27.

[37] American Psychological Association (2018).

[38] Ibid.

reported being bullied once or twice a week. 7 percent indicated they were bullied daily. **Nearly 9 percent reported being physically injured as a result of bullying.**[39]

- **Both victims and perpetrators of bullying are at a higher risk for suicide than their peers.** Children who are both victims *and* perpetrators of bullying are at the highest risk. All three groups (victims, perpetrators, and perpetrator/victims) are more likely to be depressed than children who are not involved in bullying.[40]

- In 2010 **the number of suicides in the United States was 38,364 making it the tenth leading cause of death. The number of suicides is double the number of homicides.**[41]

- **More than 800,000 people die worldwide from suicide each year**—that's one death every 40 seconds.[42]

- **More than 8 million Americans seriously consider suicide each year**, and years later say they must have been "temporarily insane."[43]

- Over the last decade, **the suicide rate among active-duty military has increased 71 percent.** Almost as many American troops (at home and abroad) have committed

---

[39] Ibid.

[40] Ibid.

[41] Crook (2004). Kindle Version, p. 1.

[42] Ibid., p. 205.

[43] Quinnett (2012) Kindle version, location 215.

suicide this year as have been killed in combat in Afghanistan.[44]

- **Experiencing child abuse, being sexually victimized by someone not in the service and exhibiting suicidal behavior before enlisting are significant risk factors for service members and veterans who attempt or commit suicide.** Suicide is the second-leading cause of death among U.S. military personnel.[45]

- **Fifteen percent of Hispanic teen girls report that they've attempted suicide**--a rate one and a half times that reported by white or black females age 12 to 17 and nearly two times that of Hispanic teen males. Yet Latinas are often the least likely to seek mental health services[46]

- **In 2014, 2,421 African Americans died by suicide in the US. Of these, 1,946 were male (80.38%).** The suicide rate of African American females was the lowest among men and women of all ethnicities.[47]

- **More than 40 percent of LGBT high school students seriously considered suicide and approximately 30 percent reported attempting suicide in the past year.** Further, compared to their heterosexual peers, LGBT high school students are up to three times more likely to report being bullied at school or online.[48]

---

[44] American Psychological Association (2010).

[45] American Psychological Association (2014).

[46] American Psychological Association (2008).

[47] American Association of Suicidology (2016).

[48] Ibid.

- A recent review of the research identified **19 studies linking suicidal behavior in lesbian, gay, and bisexual (LGB) adolescents to bullying at school,** especially among young people with "cross-gender appearance, traits, or behaviors"[49]

- **The suicide rate for American Indian youths is more than twice the national average.** "Tribal youth are raised in native families and communities subject to ongoing cultural oppression, health disparities and lack of equal access to services, lack of economic opportunity and chronic poverty."[50]

- **"Occupation is not a major predictor of suicide and it does not explain much about why the person commits suicide."**[51]

- **Suicide was the 8th leading cause of death for Asian-Americans, whereas it was the 11th leading cause of death for all racial groups combined.** Among all Asian-Americans, those aged 20-24 had the highest suicide rate.[52]

- **Suicide rates are higher in rural places than in urban places**, and this trend has been around for decades partly due to limited access to care in rural places. But even more to the fact that rural people have a greater reluctance to seek mental health care after trauma and just in general.[53]

---

[49] American Psychological Association (2018).

[50] American Psychological Association (2005).

[51] American Psychological Association (2001).

[52] American Psychological Association (2018).

[53] American Psychological Association (2017).

- A meta-analysis of 365 studies conducted over the last 50 years looking at risk factors and their ability to predict suicidal thoughts and behaviors over long periods of time analysis showed that science could only predict future suicidal thoughts and behaviors about as well as random guessing. After decades of research, science has produced no meaningful advances in suicide prediction.[54]

Contagion or "Copycat" Suicidal Behavior

Social Psychologist Ogunlade describes behavioral contagion as a "spontaneous, unsolicited and uncritical imitation of another's behavior" that occurs when certain variables are met. Those operant variables are:

1. a) the observer and the model share a similar situation or mood;

2. b) the model's behavior encourages the observer to review his condition and to change it;

3. c) the model's behavior would assist the observer to resolve a conflict by reducing restraints, if copied; and

4. d) the model is assumed to be a positive reference individual.[55]

Suicidal behavior seems to be greatly influenced by social contagion. Researcher David Phillips writes:

> Though Durkheim [the great nineteenth century sociologist] dismissed the epidemiological importance of

---

[54] Franklin et al., op. cit.
[55] Ogunlade (1979).

suggestion as a factor influencing suicide rates, reports of epidemics of suicide alarmed Europeans early in the nineteenth century at the pitch of the Romantic Movement. The English boy-poet Thomas Chatterton (1752-1770), poor and starving, swallowed arsenic and died at the age of eighteen. Alfred Victor de Vigny's sensational book *Chatterton*, dramatizing this tragic episode, was followed by a doubling of the French suicide rate between 1830 and 1840. Goethe's autobiographical *The Sorrows of Young Werther* was an enormous popular success, and it provoked imitation suicides in sufficient numbers to alarm the authorities (Fedden 1938; Alvarez 1970; Colt 1991).[56]

A century later a similar suicide cult grew in Europe between the wars—known as the *Inconnue de la Seine* (The Unknown Woman of the Seine).

> During the 1920s and early 1930s all over the Continent, nearly every student of sensibility had a plaster cast of her death mask: a young, full, sweetly smiling face which seems less dead than peacefully sleeping. The girl was in fact genuinely *inconnue*. All that is known of her is that she was fished out of the Seine and exposed on an ice block in the Paris Morgue, along with a couple of hundred other corpses awaiting identification.... She was never claimed, but someone was sufficiently impressed by her peaceful smile to take a death mask.... There is no doubt at all about the cult around her..... [A] whole generation of German girls modeled their looks on her.... Her fame was spread most effectively by a much-translated [fictionalized] best-seller, *One Unknown*, by Reinhold Conrad Muschler. He makes her an innocent young country girl who comes to Paris, falls in love with a handsome British diplomat—titled, of course—has a

---

[56] Phillips (1974).

brief but idyllic romance and then, when milord regretfully leaves to marry his suitably aristocratic English fiancée, drowns herself in the Seine. As Muschler's sales show, this was the style of explanation the public wanted for that enigmatic, dead face.... Like the Sphinx and the Mona Lisa, the power of the *Inconnue* was in her smile—subtle, oblivious, promising peace.[57]

Contagion is known to run in families. Here is a news clipping:

A FAMILY OF SUICIDES

A man named Edgar Jay Briggs, who hanged himself on his farm, near Danbury. Connecticut, a few days ago, was almost the last surviving member of a family which has practically been wiped out of existence by suicide. The history of self-destruction in this family extends over a period of more than fifty years, and in that time, so it is stated, at least twenty-one of the descendants and collaterals of the original Briggs suicide have taken their own lives. Among these were the great-grandfather, grandfather, father, brother, and two sisters of the one just dead. Many of the suicides were effected in an unusual way. One man drowned himself by holding his face in a shallow brook, another attached a weight to a collar about his neck and then waded into a pond. Others shot or hanged themselves in a way evidencing fixed determination to end their lives. All of the suicides were not blood relations, some being women who had married into the family. If the newspaper accounts, from which we have quoted, are correct, this is certainly a remarkable instance of contagion of the suicidal impulse which deserves accurate study and record.

–*Kroni Medical Record*, 60:G60601, October 20, 1901.[58]

---

[57] Miller (1992), pp 70-71.

[58] Cain (1972), frontispiece.

And then we move to teen idol contagions. When a Japanese teen idol took her life by jumping to her death, at least six teenagers also killed themselves within just a few days. Some of them also jumped to their deaths and most left a note indicating they had taken their cue from her example.[59]

The same thing happens closer to home. When one or two kids in a high school kill themselves, more kids are likely to kill themselves. And if someone in a family dies by suicide, the rest of the family members are more likely to die by suicide. Right or wrong, we all learn by example.[60]

Attractive Places for Suicide

Another aspect of contagion relates to *special attractive locations* for suicides. Since its opening in 1937, the Golden Gate Bridge has seen more than a thousand known suicides, making it the world's most popular suicide site! Throughout history certain locations have exerted a fascination for suicidal people—certain cliffs, churches, and skyscrapers. Niagara Falls, the Eiffel Tower, St. Peter's, and the Milan Cathedral have hosted many suicides. In New York in the Bowery there is a saloon with a back room where so many vagrants have killed themselves it is known as "suicide hall." In Nanjing there is the Yangtze River Bridge, in New Zealand Lawyer's Head cliff, in Japan the Aokigahara Forest at the foot of Mount Fujiyama, and the Mount Mihara island volcano near Tokyo, the Mapo Bridge in Seoul, in South India the failing farmlands, and throughout Africa stricken and impoverished

---

[59] Quinnett (2012), Kindle version, location 152.
[60] Ibid., location 173.

areas.

The suicide capital of the world is New Zealand where the Maori haven't much of a chance. And the teenage suicide capital of the world is North Dakota where teens feel so trapped that even the popular rock group Third Eye Blind visits to sing "Step back from that ledge, my friend." Needless to say, all of these locations have serious suicide prevention measures in place but regardless, people continue to jump, to hang themselves, and put bullets through their heads.

Psychologist Bruno Klopfer reports a little-known case of suicidal contagion that resulted as Hitler planned to destroy the Maginot Line by attacking Holland and Belgium.

> We know now from documentary evidence that he had an alternate plan, in case this move should fail, to march through Switzerland and attack France from the other side. The Swiss were aware of this, and hundreds of volunteers were fully prepared to destroy themselves in an attempt to blast all bridges and other forms of access into their country. It is most interesting that this was also connected with a strong religious experience. A high percentage of the Swiss population believe that what actually changed Hitler's mind and protected Switzerland from the threatened German invasion was the intervention of the only saint in their country's history, the famous Brother Klaus. There are eyewitness stories from whole battalions of Swiss militia who actually experienced the collective vision of Brother Klaus standing before them and holding the Germans off. Near the hermitage where he lived there is a monument, placed on the spot by a Swiss division, to commemorate this very experience.
>
> Whether Brother Klaus changed Hitler's mind, or whether the success of the German march through

Holland and Belgium caused him to abandon the idea of invading Switzerland, the fact remains that countless numbers of Swiss citizens would have been willing to sacrifice their lives to stop him, even temporarily. One can readily see that it makes a tremendous difference whether a suicidal act is performed under such a strong collective impulse or as an individual, personal decision, even though in each case these cultural factors will naturally play an important role. The whole sociology of suicide is one of the most fascinating areas of research.[61]

A Brief Cross-Cultural Glimpse of Suicide

NO ONE KNOWS who the first was to slash his throat with a piece of flint, take a handful of poison berries, or intentionally drop his spear to the ground in battle. Nor do we know who first jumped impulsively, or after thought, from a great cliff; walked without food into an ice storm; or stepped into the sea with no intention of coming back. Death, as Seneca states, has always lain close at hand; yet it is a mystery why the first to kill himself did: Was it a sudden impulse, or prolonged disease? An inner voice, commanding death? Perhaps shame or the threat of capture by an enemy tribe? Despair? Exhaustion? Pressure from others to spare common resources of food and land? No one knows.[62]

Certainly, cultures have varied in their notions of self-inflicted death. Several—for example, the Eskimo, Norse, Samoan, and Crow Indian—accepted, and even encouraged, "altruistic" self-sacrifice among the elderly and sick. Among the Yuit Eskimos of St. Lawrence Island, if an individual requested suicide three times, relatives were obligated to assist in the killing. The person seeking

---

[61] Klopfer (1961).

[62] Jamison (2011), Kindle version, location 161.

suicide dressed in ritual death garb and then was killed in a "destroying place" set aside specifically for that purpose. To save commonly held resources of food or to allow a nomadic society to move on unhindered by the physically ill or elderly, some societies gave tacit if not explicit approval to suicide.[63]

Mark Williams' *A Cry of Pain*

Mark Williams' *A Cry of Pain* recasts our thoughts about a cry for help in terms of a different intention:

> Suicidal behaviour is most often not a cry for help but a *cry of pain*. This idea is intended to capture the way in which an act can communicate something without communication being the main motive. It is like an animal caught in a trap, which cries with pain. The cry is brought about by the pain, but in the way it communicates distress, it changes the behaviour of other animals who hear it. And just like an animal which finds itself struggling, people who are suicidal have often been defeated by something that has happened to them. Even if there is no external evidence for such defeat, they *feel* themselves to be a loser, a failure, and responsible for the negative effects they are having on others. They come to the point where they see evidence of defeat and rejection everywhere. Periods of struggle against such feelings are punctuated by periods of inactivity and despair. ...What defeats people is not an idea about themselves, the world or the future, but a profound sense that their mental pain cannot be tolerated a moment longer.[64]

> Primo Levi speaks of anguish as a feeling we all know: Anguish is known to everyone since childhood, and everyone knows that it is often blank, undifferentiated. It

---

[63] Ibid., Location 174.

[64] Williams (1997/2014), pp. xv-xix.

rarely carries a clearly written label that also contains its motivation; when it does have one, it is often mendacious. One can believe or declare oneself to be anguished for one reason and be so due to something totally different: one can think that one is suffering at facing the future and instead be suffering because of one's past; one can think that one is suffering for others, out of pity, out of compassion, and instead be suffering for one's own reasons, more or less profound, more or less avowable and avowed; sometimes so deep that only the specialist, the analyst of souls, knows how to exhume them....The central idea of *Cry of Pain* is that although many factors contribute to suicide, it represents a reaction to a feeling of being defeated combined with a feeling of not being able to escape the consequences of defeat. Like the animal caught in a trap, the struggle to get free is followed by defeat and hopelessness.[65]

David Webb and the Suicide Imperative

David Webb describes the imperative feeling of suicidality:

I'm sure you know this feeling but I invite you to do it now. Just hold your breath until you start to really need to take a breath. Then keep holding it a bit longer ... then a bit more. You will reach a point where you absolutely must take a breath. Your whole body will be demanding that you take in some air. Don't injure yourself, but, if you can, hold your breath just a little longer. The demand for air will become all-important. It will dominate your consciousness. Everything else in your life will become irrelevant. You are obsessed with the desire for some air. Don't overdo it, but for those of you who have never experienced a serious drug addiction, that all-consuming craving, then this little exercise will give you some idea.... I do not see suicidality as immoral, certainly not a sin. I

---

[65] Ibid., p. 228.

never have and I doubt if I ever will. It has always seemed a perfectly legitimate option that everyone undeniably has available to them. Of course, I would much prefer it that no one, including myself, felt such despair that they chose to exercise this option, and I would like to do whatever I can to prevent people, including myself, from reaching such a point of despair. But suicide has always made sense to me. It still does.[66]

David Lester has pointed out that suicidologists have generally concluded that many attempted suicides are not actually trying to die since the gestures are weak—taking less than a lethal dose, cutting lightly and so forth. These seemingly instrumental gestures that are often interpreted as a cry for help or an interpersonal manipulation of some sort are now being referred to as "parasuicides" or "self-poisoners" and "self-injurers".[67,68] Lester considers the effects various forms of oppression—actual and internalized—have on their victims.[69] He proposed a general social conflict theory of suicide in which suicide can be conceptualized as a political act and is hypothesized to be a reaction against oppression. He cites Hendin as arguing that suicide in African Americans must be understood in light of the society's overt rejection leaving many trapped in unbearable life situations by their lack of education, lack of job opportunities, and the destructive effect of ghetto life.[70] Lester further cites Stephens as examining the role of interpersonal relationships of modern

---

[66] Webb (2010), pp. 28-30.

[67] Lester (2004), p. 21.

[68] The term *parasuicidal* is credited to Kleitman et al. (1969).

[69] Lester (1990).

[70] Hendin (1969).

American women in their suicidal behavior and concluded that their social and psychological experiences prepared them to be victims—victims of parents, of men, and of relationships in which the self is continually mortified.[71]

Ronald Maris maintains that virtually everyone engaged in suicidology agrees that the descriptive profiles of self-destructive behaviors of the past must give way to "dynamic *developmental* models". "Suicidality varies over time and among different types of individuals. It is argued here that *the suicide's biography or "career"* is always relevant to his or her self-destructive reaction to crisis and that it is precisely this history, individual or group, which tends to be neglected." [emphasis added][72] *"Suicide is one product of a gradual loss of hope and the will and resources to live, a kind of running down and out of life energies, a bankruptcy of psychic defenses against death and decay."*[73] Maris concludes,

> ...it would appear that at least in the immediate surround of suicide, instead of clear-headed decisions, we find disorganization, disequilibrium, and disintegration of self and social supports (Litman 1967; Perlin 1975). Perhaps some of these traits are a function of the oft-cited ambivalence that accompanies both suicide and depression (Freud 1940; Menninger 1938). Many suicides wish to live *if* their physical or emotional anguish would abate, *if* their marriage could be saved, *if* their depression would stop recurring, *if*, in sum, they could have genuine hope of feeling better short of death. Neuringer has observed that these contingencies for suicides frequently have a "if-and-only-if" character. That

---

[71] Stephens (1988).

[72] Maris (1981).

[73] Ibid., p. 69.

is, eventual suicides suffer from cognitive and perceptual constriction (1964). It has been argued that emotionally, suicides have pathological, narcissistic ideals. If they cannot achieve them–and almost by definition their goals are unobtainable–they feel they have no choice except to die (Bonime 1965).[74]

"The *fantasy of being rescued* in suicide" by Viggo Jensen and Thomas Petty is a complex psychoanalytic construction much deserving our attention and tracing ego splitting back to early Freud and his later "Mourning and Melancholia". From the editor's introduction: "Suicide is dyadic; fusion fantasies and self-object confusion lie at its heart, and in almost all instances, a warning is given before the deadly chance is taken. Jensen and Petty show how playing the odds with death almost always involves a test for the person who is cast in the role of potential rescuer: "Which is it to be," the attempter unconsciously asks, "Will you save me from death and demonstrate your love, or will you abandon me to death, and demonstrate your aversion?" This phenomenon is of great importance in the treatment of suicidal patients because so commonly the therapist is the chosen rescuer or abandoner, and will almost always be tested in this way at some critical moment of psychotherapy...." The authors summarize their conclusions:

> The fantasy of being rescued from suicide is expressed as a suicidal attempt so arranged that it invites the intervention of a particular rescuer to prevent its successful execution. A wish to be saved is an element in every attempted suicide. The rescuer is chosen from among those who have the capacity to empathize with the suicidal person at a particular time. In 'borderline' and psychotic individuals the choice may be symbolic

---

[74] Ibid., p. 292.

and vaguely expressed.... *The prototype for the relationship the suicidal person seeks with the rescuer probably is that early one between child and parent when they shared a common ego and responded directly to the unconscious of each other.* The rescuer must have a surplus of free libidinal energy with which to love the suicidal person and initiate the rescue, and he must have sufficient ego strength to deal with the sum of the suicidal person's and his own destructive impulses. Often a potential rescuer recognizes the appeal to him but disregards it because of his own hostility or lack of ego strength and libidinal resources....The more conscious the fantasy of rescue, the easier it is for the suicidal person to find and accept a rescuer....*The fantasy is an attempt to restore the original relationship between the primal object and the ego of the suicidal person* (emphasis added).[75]

James Hillman's Four Root Metaphors for Considering Suicide

Jungian Analyst James Hillman in his remarkable book, Suicide and the Soul, points out that there are four root metaphors that have governed the traditional studies of suicide in Western civilization and that the late arriving psychological perspective stands as a challenge to these four pillars of thought.[76] They are:

1.   *Sociological*
The root metaphor which governs the sociologist's attitudes and to which he gives his loyalty is Society. Society is a living reality for him. It provides a way of understanding himself; it offers a model of thought from which he can deduce hypotheses, and a field of facts

---

[75] Jensen & Petty (1996), pp. 131-141.
[76] Hillman (1965/2011).

where the hypotheses can be tested and applied. New facts will be first related to this model, and the better they can be taken up by it, the more effective the sociologist.[77]

2. *Legal*

Turning to the legal point of view towards suicide, we find it declared criminal by three of the great traditions upon which Western justice stands: Roman law, Church law, and English law. In 1809 Blackstone stated in the fifteenth edition of his *Commentaries* that because suicide is against God and King "the law has therefore ranked this among the highest crimes."

Until 1870 the deterrent against suicide in English law was mainly against the physical property of the deceased rather than against the physical body. The property of those who committed suicide while of sound mind was declared forfeit to the crown. Until 1961 English law still held that the estate of the deceased could be penalised; life insurance was not paid out to the benefactors.[78]

3. *Theological*

The word of God and religion is authoritative. When you or I consider taking our lives, listening in our own ways to God, we no longer follow authority. We set ourselves up as theologians. We are studying God independently. This can well lead to religious delusions and to theological anarchy, with each man having his own God, his own sect, his own theology. *Theology would have us believe that God can speak only through the events of fortune, because death may come only from without.* Again, as with sociology and law, death must be exogenous, visited upon us through the world: enemy,

---

[77] Ibid., pp 25f.
[78] Ibid., pp 26f.

accident, or disease.[79]

4.   *Medicine*

The primary caution of the physician is *primum nihil nocere*— above all, to harm nothing. His tasks are to prevent illness; to treat, heal, and cure where possible; to comfort always; to repair and encourage; to allay pain; to discover and fight disease—all in order to promote physical wellbeing, that is, life. Anything against these aims must be opposed, because it endangers the root metaphor: promoting life...The medical model itself supports the standard rule: any indication of suicide, any threat of death, calls for the immediate action of locks and drugs and constant surveillance— treatment usually reserved for criminals.[80]

Hillman's psychological stance is:

The models from which those four fields having most to do with suicide regard the problem are of no help to the analyst. All of them prejudge suicide, partly because suicide threatens the root metaphors upon which they stand. Therefore, all share certain traits in common. Their main concern is with suicide prevention because their models are tinged with a dread of death. This dread arises from their not having adequate place for death within their present models of thought. They conceive death as exogenous to life, not as something lodged in the soul, not as a continuous possibility and choice. By admitting this they would be admitting suicide, thereby threatening their own foundations. Neither Society, nor Law, nor Church, nor Life would then be safe.... If suicide prevention is a prejudgment and an analyst opposes it on the grounds that it does not lead to understanding

<hr>

[79] Ibid., p. 32.
[80] Ibid., pp. 32f.

suicide as a psychological fact, this in no way implies that one is therefore 'for suicide'. Again, *the issue is not for or against suicide, but what it means in the psyche....*

The analytical view will have to arise independently of these four fields because suicide shows this independence of the psyche from society, law, theology, and even from the life of the body. Suicide is such a threat to them not only because it pays no heed to the cautions of their traditions and opposes their root metaphors, but largely because it asserts radically the independent reality of the soul.[81]

---

[81] Ibid., pp. 36f.

Chapter Four

The Major Psychological Perspectives on Suicide

The Freudian Approach

Any survey of the psychoanalytic tradition necessarily begins with Sigmund Freud's 1917 paper "Mourning and Melancholia" in which he contrasts normal and ordinary grief reactions to loss (mourning) with chronic and debilitating mental preoccupations (melancholia or what we now refer to as Major Depression).[82]

As discussed earlier in the presentation of the Relational Listening approach, Freud's thinking revolved around his understanding of a an essential "split" in the sense of personal agency, "the I" (translated as "ego"), such that we might speak of a "me-self" and an "other-self". That is, the nature of *personal agency* is such that *we perceive and act with one part of ourselves—our "me-self" or primary I—while what we perceive and act upon becomes known, is represented, taken in, owned, or identified with as another part of ourselves—our "other-self."*

Much of the time in early life and throughout our lives the "other self" is greeted by "the primary I" with hostility because it somehow stands in the way of primary ego pleasuring motives. Metaphorically, as long as the breast behaves according to my wishes and commands it is simply another aspect of myself. But when the breast is slow, cantankerous, unreliable or a problem otherwise, frustration and anger with resultant aggression toward

---

[82] S. Freud (1917), 14:237-258.

the uncooperative breast emerge and I have to figure out how to deal with this unwanted otherness and my exploring and figuring of the external otherness results in an internalized representation or mapping of what's out there giving me problems. *Perceptual, motor, and cognitive exploring, figuring, and representing results in an internal representation or identification with the frustrating otherness that is imbued with anger and aggression because it is not under the sway of my primary pleasuring ego.* This means that at times our other-self is experienced as angry or depriving or abusive toward our primary self, while at other times it is our me-self that is angry at the uncooperative internalized otherness—an otherness that is often dealt with by denying and projecting it onto real others in our external world—"It's not me that's a problem but you because....". So later in life in any given engagement with others it may be our primary other expressing anger at a projected inner otherness or the other way around: an introjected angry other shouting at the externally projected me-self. We will talk more about this role-reversal in relational experiences later.

According to Freud, in ordinary *mourning* the normally functioning ego has suffered a loss with grief and, after having painfully accepted the reality of that loss, matures—expands its purview—through creating memorials as well as locating and identifying with others in order to repair or replace that loss. In *melancholia* the primary ego discharges its aggression toward the internalized, identified ego part representing the failing and lost primary internalized object and, being so preoccupied is unable to create living memorials or accept the reality of the loss and cannot move on to repair or replace that loss.

Freud's formulation reads that that the ego turns aggression against itself—that is, the primary ego discharges its aggression toward the identificatory ego resulting in a debilitating depressive reaction often defended against by denial and projection and/or manic activity that works as a defense against depressive hopelessness and despair. That is, the me-self is now endlessly caught up in helpless and hopeless persecutory experiencing and/or endless attack upon that persecutory other-self. When the melancholic reaction is chronic and severe we have the foundation for a life-long "suicidal career"—an internalized character reaction—a shut-down—in reaction to "the slings and arrows of outrageous fortune" that produces a cascade of different kinds of self-injuring, self-destructive and/or high risk behaviors. Even if relatively favorable developmental experiences follow so that the person develops intellectually, creatively, and relationally fairly well, the helpless-hopeless-despairing foundation of the traumatized split ego at traumatizing moments may re-assert itself, i.e., be transferred into current relationships creating an inexorable agonizing shut-down experiences—a call of darkness, the compulsion to stop consciousness in order to stop the pain.

At this point I want to insert my formulations from earlier in the book characterizing different kinds of reactions if the internalization is transferred from *"Organizing"* connecting-disconnecting relatedness possibilities or if the reactions are transferred from the *"Symbiotic"* attachment-abandonment relatedness possibilities. I have said that I believe the *"Organizing"* transfers are more likely to lead to the total darkness of suicide, while the "Symbiotic" transfers are more likely to lead to instrumental or unconsciously manipulative interpersonal activities to get one's emotional (dependency) needs met.

Suicide was known to Freud from the earliest "specimen case" of psychoanalysis, *Anna O.*, who had made a suicide attempt and sought therapy shortly after nursing her father to death. Throughout his writings Freud mentions suicide in many contexts but leaves clear-cut formulations to later generations of writers.

In *The Psychopathology of Everyday Life* (1901), Freud expresses his view that the trend to self-destruction over a lifetime may manifest as either conscious or unconscious intention.

> There is no need to think such self-destruction rare, for the trend to self- destruction is present to a certain degree in very many more human beings than those in whom it is carried out. Self-injuries are, as a rule, a compromise between this instinct and the forces that are still working against it, and even when suicide actually results the inclination to suicide will have been present for a long time before in less strength, or in the form of an unconscious and suppressed trend.....Even a *conscious* intention of committing suicide chooses its times, means, and opportunity; and it is quite in keeping with this that an *unconscious* intention should wait for a precipitating occasion, which can take over a part of the causation and by engaging the subject's defensive forces, can liberate the intention from their pressure."[83]

At meetings of the Vienna Psychoanalytical Society on April 20 and 27, 1910, there was a discussion of suicide in which Adler and Steckel spoke to the aggressive aspects of suicide. Freud remained silently thoughtful until it was time for a summing up:

> I have an impression that in spite of all the valuable material that has been brought before us in this

---

[83] S. Freud (1901), 6:178-185.

discussion, we have not reached a decision on the problem that interests us. We are anxious, above all, to know how it becomes possible for the extraordinarily powerful life instinct to be overcome; whether this can only come about with the help of a disappointed libido or whether the ego can renounce its self-preservation for its own egoistic motives. It may be that we have failed to answer this psychological question because we have no adequate means of approaching it. We can, I think, only take as our starting point the condition of melancholia which is so familiar to us clinically and a comparison between it and the affect of mourning. The affective processes in melancholia, however, and the vicissitudes undergone by the libido in that condition are totally unknown to us. Nor have we arrived at a psychoanalytic understanding of the chronic affect of mourning. Let us suspend our judgment until experience has solved this problem.[84]

Seven years later in "Mourning and Melancholia" Freud addressed his questions regarding the problem of Melancholia which today is generally referred to as Major Depression. This passage refers to the splitting of the ego—a process discussed earlier:

We see how in him one part of the ego sets itself over and against the other, judges it critically and in a word takes it as its object. Our suspicion that the critical agency which is here split off from the ego might also show its independence in other circumstances will be confirmed by every other observation.[85]

In 1920 Freud again considers suicide in the context of a case study of an 18-year-old girl, who was brought to Freud by her

---

[84] S. Freud (1910), 11:232.
[85] S. Freud (1917), 14:247-252.

father about six months after she made a suicide attempt.

> Analysis has explained the enigma of suicide in the following way: Probably no one finds the mental energy required to kill himself unless, in the first place, in doing so, he is at the same time killing an object with whom he has identified himself and, in the second place, is turning against himself a death wish which had been directed against someone else. Nor need the regular discovery of these unconscious death wishes in those who have attempted suicide surprise us (any more than it ought to make us think that it confirms our deductions), since the unconscious of all human beings is full enough of such death wishes against even those they love.[86]

Robert Litman, in his comprehensive review of Freud's ideas on suicide, interprets this passage:

> The most significant of the ideas expressed above is the discovery that suicide is multiply determined by the interaction of several motives. The emphasis is on ego-splitting and identifications. The suicidal act is explained [in this case] as a reenactment, by a split-off ego identification with mother, of the delivery of the brother.... The most important of these for psychoanalysis is the 'negative therapeutic reaction.'[87] *Some [people] inevitably respond to good news, congratulations, or progress in analysis, by increased anxiety, depression, or self-injury* (emphasis added).[88]

> Judged by all their actions the instinct of self-preservation has been reversed. They seem to aim at nothing other than self-injury and self-destruction. It is possible, too, that the people who in fact do, in the end, commit suicide, belong to this group.... Patients of this

---

[86] S. Freud (1920), 18:147-172.

[87] S. Freud (1923), 19:49.

[88] Litman (1996).

kind are not able to tolerate recovery toward treatment and fight against it with all their strength.[89]

Concludes Litman:

> To Freud, suicide represented a symptom of what we suffer from, a product of man and his civilization, a consequence of mental trends which can be found to some degree in every human being.... Experience has confirmed Freud's statement that each suicide is multiply determined by the interaction of several motives. Suicide is by no means a homogeneous or unitary piece of human behavior. On the contrary, suicide comprises a variety of behaviors with many important aspects--historical, legal, social, and philosophical, as well as medical and psychological. The psychoanalytic explanations of the psychopathology of suicide are complex, multidimensional and, at some points, ambiguous and redundant....
>
> My experience is in agreement with Freud's general schematic view. Deep down, there is a suicidal trend in all of us. This self-destructiveness is tamed, controlled, and overcome through our healthy identifications, ego defenses, and constructive habits of living and loving. When the ordinary defenses, controls, and ways of living and loving break down, the individual may easily be forced into a suicidal crisis. At such times he feels helpless, hopeless, and abandoned and may or may not be aware of a great deal of inexpressible, aggressive tension.[90]

Following Freud's "Mouring and Melancholia", the next major addition to psychoanalytic thinking on suicide was made by Karl Menninger in 1933 that emphasizes unconscious motivations.

---

[89] S. Freud (1940), 23:148-150.

[90] Litman, op. cit., pp. 337-339

The conception of self-destruction as a flight from reality, from ill-health, disgrace, poverty and the like, is seductive because of its simplicity.... Its essential fallacy is one of incompleteness; it lies in the implied assumption that the forces impelling the regression come wholly from without....From the standpoint of analytical psychology the push is more important than the pull, i.e. the ego is driven by more powerful forces than external reality. The paramount factors in determining behaviour are the impulses from within, the motives originating in the individual which express his attempt at adjustment to reality.[91]

Menninger goes ahead to describe what Maris has later called a "suicidal career", that is, the life-long patterns of self-destruction that lead to later attempts and later suicides.

For we know that the individual always, in a measure, creates his own environment, and thus the suicidal person must help to create the very thing from which, in suicide, he takes flight. If we are to explain the act dynamically, therefore, we are compelled to seek an explanation for the wish to put oneself in a predicament from which one cannot, except by suicide, escape. In other words *if, for one's own unconscious purposes, one brings about an apparent justification in external reality for self-destruction, the unconscious purposes are of more significance in understanding suicide than the apparently simple, inevitable external realities* (emphasis added).[92]

Menninger concludes with his famous three elements of suicide:

We must think of suicide, then, as a peculiar kind of death which entails *three elements: the element of dying,*

---

[91] Menninger (1933), Kindle version, locations 32-35.
[92] Ibid., location 40.

the element of killing, and the element of being killed. Each element requires separate analysis. Each is an act for which there exist motives, unconscious and conscious. The latter are usually evident enough; the unconscious motives are now our chief consideration.[93]

Sociologists Spaulding and Simpson in sympathy with the psychoanalytic point of view, further echo the factors going into what Maris calls "the suicide career."

The most widely accepted view today in psychoanalysis is that suicide is most often a form of "displacement"; that is, the desire to kill someone who has thwarted the individual is turned back on the individual himself. Or technically stated: the suicide murders the introjected object and expiates guilt for wanting to murder the object. The ego is satisfied and the superego mollified through self-murder.... All of the emotions manifested in suicides are, then, explicable in terms of the life-history of the individual, particularly the channeling of the basic psychic configurations through the family. It may thus be possible to do what Durkheim thought was impossible— namely, classify suicides originally in terms of motives and what he calls morphologically.[94]

Mark Williams, countering the emphasis on aggression in suicide, believes there are other important motivations:

Patients speak about a wish to join a dead relative with whom they identify strongly. These reunion fantasies are not readily explained simply on the basis of self-directed aggression. They appear to result from libidinal rather than aggressive wishes, pleasurable rather than masochistic fantasies. Other patients have fantasies about rebirth following their own death, a rebirth they

---

[93] Ibid., location 46.
[94] Spaulding et al. (2005). Kindle version, locations 268-271.

can hasten by destroying this self.... Still others appear to be looking for a sense of mastery, or even omnipotence, over an impossible situation, and their death is the only element in life that they feel they have retained control over. Some believe they will still, in some sense, be present after their death to 'see what happens next', and, in a spirit of revenge that is sometimes present as part of suicidal thoughts, able to experience pleasure in the distress their death might cause others. The inconsistency between death as escape into oblivion and a continued existence in which the pain of others can be experienced is not apparent to the suicidal person in their confusion.[95]

In 1961's *The Cry for Help*, Norman Farberow and Edwin Shneidman, while generally endorsing the motives of aggression and escape, point to other possible motivations and list what are the particular aspects of suicide:

(A) its drastic nature;...

(B) its gamble with success;...

(C) its comic-tragedy aspects in failure;...

(D) its mobilization of guilt, death wishes, or fears in others;...

(E) its primitive character as motoric behavior; the individual, in developing from id response, first uses motor activity automatically for discharge of his tensions and gratification of his needs. With growth he learns to insert a time period between stimulus and reaction; an acquisition of certain tension tolerance is necessary to bind primitive reaction impulses. Reality judgment is necessary. For all of this a more mature, rational, less narcissistic ego is required, which is not present in the

---

[95] Williams, pp. 126f.

suicidal patient. The suicide fears the experience of further traumatic states.[96]

Gains picks up on a very important aspect involved in complete mourning which Freud alludes to—*identification as an ego-building process* creating in the individual a sense of continuity with life.

> In psychoanalytic theory, the essential work of mourning has been defined as the acceptance of the irrevocability of the loss, and the progressive cathexis of the lost object, which frees the mourner to make new relationships and find new satisfactions. This is the detachment task of mourning. From this perspective, pathological or incomplete mourning results from an inability to relinquish the object, with consequent denial of the finality of the loss and unconscious fantasies of undoing and reunion.... Emphasis on the need to detach from the lost object has obscured another aspect of the work of mourning, which is to repair the disruption to the inner self-other relationship caused by the actual loss. *The individual needs to reconnect the severed bond, now on an exclusively internal basis, and to maintain the availability of a sustaining inner relationship. This is the task I call "creating continuity."* The mourner is thus faced with the difficult project of simultaneously making room for new investments while consolidating the old (emphasis added)....[97]

> [Freud] moved beyond the exclusive focus on detachment and toward recognition of the task of continuity. This came about through his growing appreciation of the role of identification. In "Mourning and Melancholia" (1917), Freud contrasted normal mourning, where detachment takes place, with

---

[96] Farberow & Shneidman (1961), p. 176.

[97] Gaines (1997), Kindle version, locations 10-14.

depression (melancholia), where identification with the ambivalently regarded object occurs. Later Freud realized that identification is not a pathological process, but occurs normally as a mechanism to help the child adapt to changes and losses in the relation to his parents, and is actually one of the major ways in which development occurs (Freud 1921, 1923). Later still, Freud (1933) indicated his awareness that identification can also be part of mourning, stating, "If one has lost an object or has been obliged to give it up, one often compensates oneself by identifying oneself with it and by setting it up once more in one's ego, so that here object choice regresses, as it were, to identification."[98]

Gains calls our attention to some elegant work of Anna Freud in which she autobiographically recounts her difficulties in mourning over the death of her father and that only after allowing herself to identify fully with his intellectual prowess as well as his dynamic leadership could she achieve continuity with her life and allow herself to come into her own as a brilliant writer and theoretician as well as a powerful and dynamic leader of the psychoanalytic movement.[99]

The Jungian Approach

The Jungian Analytic perspective centers around what life and *death as a part of life* has meant to people from all cultures throughout time. And how those meanings have been expressed in archetypal forms—notably in sleep and death. A key distinction made by Jungians is between an individual self and a collective or spiritual Self to which there is both a light and dark side. "When

---

[98] Ibid., location 84.

[99] A. Freud (1967).

the dark side prevails, a situation in which death seems more desirable or less horrifying than life occurs. This state, in fact, is a necessary, although not a sufficient, prerequisite for any suicidal act.[100]

Carl Jung wrote: "The negation of life's fulfillment is synonymous with the refusal to accept its ending. Both mean not wanting to live; not wanting to live is identical with not wanting to die. Waxing and waning make one curve. Whenever possible, our consciousness refuses to accommodate itself to this undeniable truth."[101]

Jungian Bruno Klopfer considers six situations in which death seems preferable to life, whether rational or irrational:

1. *The death of the hero or martyr* is the most common and well-known of these situations, in which the life of the individual seems far less important than the preservation of the ideal.

2. *Intractable pain or unbearable mental anguish* make life seem so miserable that death appears largely as a liberation, regardless of what expectation a person may have regarding the hereafter.

3. *Counterphobic reaction to death* is closely related to the situation described above, in which the expectation of death seems so unbearable that the individual prefers an end to horror to a horror without end....

4. *Reunion with a dead loved one* is sought in cases where the death of a loved one seems to carry with it all the meaning of life. The desire to reunite with this person in death becomes so overwhelming that it

---

[100] Klopfer (1961). In Farberow & Shneidman (1961), pp. 193-203.
[101] Jung (1959).

does not even matter whether the individual has any concrete notion of how this reunion will take place.

5. *The search for freedom*, one of the most peculiar of these situations, leads to cases of completely unpredictable, almost whimsical acts of suicide, involving the desire not to be committed, not to be tied down, to life or anything it contains.

6. *The search for closure*, the opposite situation, is an older person's longing for death as a well-deserved closure to a rich and full life.[102]

The Jungian perspective highlights an often unconscious feature of a person with suicidal tendencies—the search for "re-birth" or "re-generation" in the broadest spiritual sense.

The principle of dying and being reborn belongs to the essence of the unfolding life process.... In the present context, rebirth implies a spiritual rebirth experienced within the life span of the individual....The archetypal symbol of the night journey of the hero, connected with the daily experience of the rising and setting sun, is the most general representation of this principle. Jung likes to compare the decisive phase in the analytic process of self-realization with the symbol of crucifixion. Death in this connection is clearly conceived as the death of the ego that has lost contact with the self and thus with the meaning of life. The ego has to return to the womb of the magna mater to reestablish this contact and to be reborn with a new meaning for life.... This process of rebirth is not without danger. The archetypal force of the magna mater has both life-giving and life-destroying aspects, parallel to the dark and bright side of the Self. Therefore, the night journey contains always the danger of ending in destruction rather than in rebirth. If the patient is made aware of this danger and is helped to face it by the

[102] Klopfer, op. cit., pp. 195f.

analyst, the suicidal crisis can be transformed into a profoundly healing and life-giving experience....

This explains the negative correlation between the tendency to suicide and the degree of self-realization or self-actualization reached by a person within his lifetime. The less successful a person is in being or becoming himself, the more vital energy he invests in what Jung calls the persona; the need to play a certain role, to act as one thinks other persons expect one to act. Thus, the greater will be the need for psychological rebirth when this persona-centered existence reaches the end of its usefulness.[103]

In my research into suicidality perhaps the most profound book I encountered was James Hillman's *Suicide and the Soul* where he makes clear that death is an important aspect of life and that the question of how one lives or dies—by fate or by choice is a crucial one everyone must consider.

Any careful consideration of life entails reflections of death, and the confrontation with reality means facing mortality. We never come fully to grips with life until we are willing to wrestle with death. We need not postulate a death drive nor need we speculate about death and its place in the scheme of things to make a simple point: every deep and complex concern, whether in oneself or with another, has in it the problem of death. And the problem of death is posed most vividly in suicide. Nowhere else is death so near. If we want to move towards self-knowledge and the experience of reality, then an enquiry into suicide becomes the first step.[104]

Hillman speaks to the position of the analyst:

When suicide is the problem of the hour an analyst

---

[103] Ibid., pp. 196-197.
[104] Hillman (1965), p. 15.

should be expected to have achieved a conscious point of view beyond his subjective concerns. But how does an analyst develop objectivity about suicide?... Objectivity means openness; and openness about suicide is not easily gained. The law has found it criminal, religion calls it a sin, and society turns away from it. It has been long the habit to hush it up or excuse it by insanity, as if it were the primary anti-social aberration. Objectivity here puts one immediately outside the collective. Openness to suicide means more than taking an individual stand against collective moral opinion. An objective enquiry in this field somehow betrays the impulse of life itself. The question raised in this enquiry necessarily leads beyond the touch of life. But only death is beyond the touch of life, so that openness to suicide means first of all a movement towards death, openly and without dread.[105]

Hillman emphasizes not only the need for analysts to be objective about death and suicide but *to enter into a committed relationship with the person to the extent one is also a participant in the tension of the unfolding process.*

This tension of body and soul is crystallised most clearly in the problem of suicide. Here, the body can be destroyed by a 'mere fantasy'. No other question forces us so acutely into facing the reality of the psyche as a reality equal to the body. And because all analysis turns on the axis of psychic reality, suicide becomes the paradigmatic experience of all analysis, perhaps of all life.[106]

Hillman speaks of suicide prevention as an antithesis of the experience of death the person is needing to have, a stance that precludes exploration. "If suicide prevention is a prejudgment and

---

[105] Ibid., p. 16.
[106] Ibid., p. 23.

an analyst opposes it on the grounds that it does not lead to understanding suicide as a psychological fact, this in no way implies that one is therefore 'for suicide.' Again, the issue is not for or against suicide, but what it means in the psyche."[107]

The concern of an analyst is to maintain connection with the inside of experience and not to surrender to the pressures of the outside.

> *If an analyst wants to understand something going on in the soul he may never proceed in an attitude of prevention....*Not prevention, but confirmation, is the analyst's approach to experience. His desire is to give recognition to the states of the soul which the person concerned is undergoing, so that they may become realized in the personality and be lived consciously. He is there to confirm what is going on—whatever is going on. Ideally, he is not there to approve, to blame, to alter, or to prevent. He may search for meaning, but this is to explore the given, not to lead away from the experience as it is."[108]

In Hillman's view psychotherapy is aimed at understanding the depth of psyche that includes not only personal history experiences but collective archetypal experiences.

> Psychology means 'logos of psyche', the speech or telling of the soul. As such, psychology is necessarily depth psychology, since, as we have seen above, soul refers to the inner, the deep.
>
> And the logic of psychology is necessarily the method of understanding which tells of the soul and speaks to the soul in its own language. *The deeper a psychology can go*

---

[107] Ibid., P. 37.

[108] Ibid., p 47f.

with its understanding, i.e., into universal inner meanings expressed by the archetypal speech of mythical 'tellings', the more scientifically accurate it is on the one hand and the more soul it has on the other.[109]

Hillman specifies the ideal position of the analyst: "Without dread, without the prejudices of prepared positions, without a pathological bias, suicide becomes 'natural'. It is natural because it is a possibility of our nature, a choice open to each human psyche. The analyst's concern is less with the suicidal choice as such, than it is with helping the other person to understand the meaning of this choice, *the only one which asks directly for the death experience.*"[110]

Echoing the findings of Durkheim and other sociologists Hillman focuses on freedom of choice.

> A main meaning of the choice is the importance of death for individuality. As individuality grows so does the possibility of suicide. Sociology and theology recognize this, as we have seen. Where man is law unto himself, responsible to himself for his own actions (as in the culture of cities, in the unloved child, in protestant areas, in creative people), the choice of death becomes a more frequent alternative. In this choice of death, of course, the opposite lies concealed. Until we can choose death, we cannot choose life. *Until we can say no to life, we have not really said yes to it,* but have only been carried along by its collective stream. The individual standing against this current experiences death as the first of all alternatives, for he who goes against the stream of life is its opponent and has become identified with death. Again, the death experience is needed to separate from the collective flow

---

[109] Ibid., p. 51.
[110] Ibid., p. 62.

of life and to discover individuality. To understand all these death patterns, analysis cannot turn anywhere but to the soul to see what it says about death. Analysis develops its ideas on death empirically from the soul itself. Again Jung has been the pioneer. He simply listened to the soul tell its experiences and watched the images of the goal of life which the living psyche produces out of itself. Here, he was neither philosopher, nor physician, nor theologian, but psychologist, student of the soul. He discovered that death has many guises and that it does not usually appear in the psyche as death *per se*, as extinction, negation, and finality. Images of dying and ideas of death have quite other meanings in dreams and fantasies. The soul goes through many death experiences, yet physical life goes on; and as physical life comes to a close, the soul often produces images and experiences that show continuity.[111]

The therapeutic action or transformation "begins at this point where there is no hope. Despair produces the cry for salvation, for which hope would be too optimistic, too confident.... My only certainty is my suffering which I ask to be taken from me by dying. An animal awareness of suffering, and full identification with it, becomes the humiliating ground of transformation."[112]

Hillman confidently concludes: "This emphasis on experience, this loyalty to the soul and the dispassionate scientific objectivity towards its phenomena, and this affirmation of the analytical relationship may release the transformation the soul has been seeking. It may come only at the last minute. It may never come at all. But there is no other way."[113]

---

[111] Ibid., p. 64f.
[112] Ibid., p. 65.
[113] Ibid.

The Shneidman Approach

Introducing Shneidman as the widely acclaimed foremost expert on suicide is the father of a young man who was a physician and an attorney and who had taken his life.

In 1949, Shneidman was asked to look at a pair of suicide notes and communicate to the widows of the men who had written them. The experience of the suicide notes, back in 1949, was so remarkable to Shneidman that he and his colleagues, Dr. Norman Farberow and Dr. Robert Litman, did the first study on suicide notes following scientific protocols. Shneidman, with his colleagues Litman and Farberow, founded the Los Angeles Suicide Prevention Center. Shneidman went on to develop a program in suicide prevention for the National Institute of Mental Health, and, eventually, to teach, write, study, and publish a number of books about suicide and contribute to many more, as well as to write seven pages of text on suicide for the 1973 edition of the *Encyclopedia Britannica*.[114]

By 1998 Shneidman had made a major impact on the field of suicidology and he had grasped the folly of many of the early approaches. He wrote:

> Our best route to understanding suicide is not through the study of the structure of the brain, nor the study of social statistics, nor the study of mental diseases, but directly through the study of human emotions described in plain English, in the words of the suicidal person. The most important question to a potentially suicidal person is not an inquiry about family history or laboratory tests of blood or spinal fluid, but "Where do you hurt?" and

---

[114] *Encyclopedia Britannica* (1973).

"How can I help you?[115]

Shneidman had come to understand that the lingua franca for studying suicide was the language of ordinary everyday words that are found in the verbatim narratives of those who suffer the pain and anguish of suicidality. The words convey the frustrated human needs—the drama of the *mind*. "In almost every case, suicide is caused by pain, a certain kind of pain, psychological pain, which I call Psycheache."[116] David Webb in his moving account of his own suicidal career mentions that Shneidman in a conversation with him spoke of *a pressing need for a phenomenology of suicide, for a study of what it feels like to be suicidal.*[117]

Shneidman speaks of all the pain in life's dark and unhappy moments when we feel upset, disturbed and perturbed. Sometimes the pain is physical but more often it is psychological pain—a phenomenon of the human *mind* that other species lack. He held that psychological pain was the fundamental ingredient of suicide.

> A basic rule for us to keep in mind is: We can reduce the lethality if we lessen the anguish, the perturbation. Suicidal individuals who are asked "Where do you hurt?" intuitively know that this is a question about their emotions and their lives, and they answer appropriately, not in biological terms, but with some literary or humanistic sophistication, in psychological terms. What I mean by this is to ask about the person's feelings,

---

[115] Shneidman (2004), Kindle version, location 60.
[116] Ibid., location 81.
[117] Webb (2010), p. 92.

worries, and pain....[118]

Suicide happens when the Psycheache is deemed unbearable and death is actively sought to stop the unceasing flow of painful consciousness. Suicide is a tragic drama in the mind.[119]

Shneidman lists his now widely acclaimed "Ten Commonalities Found in Suicide":[120]

1. *The common purpose of suicide is to seek a solution.* Suicide is not a random act. It is never done without purpose.

2. *The common goal of suicide is cessation of consciousness.* Suicide is best understood as moving toward the complete stopping of one's consciousness and unendurable pain, especially when cessation is seen by the suffering person as the solution, indeed the perfect solution of life's painful and pressing problems.

3. *The common stimulus in suicide is psychological pain.* If cessation is what the suicidal person is moving toward, psychological pain (or Psycheache) is what the person is seeking to escape.

4. *The common stressor in suicide is frustrated psychological needs.* In general, human acts are intended to satisfy a variety of human needs.

5. *The common emotion in suicide is hopelessness-helplessness.* At the beginning of life, the infant experiences a number of emotions (rage, bliss) that quickly become differentiated.

---

[118] Shneidman, op. cit., location 111.
[119] Ibid., location 164.
[120] Ibid., locations 1300-1353. The items here are partial quotes from his list.

In the adolescent or adult suicidal state, the pervasive feeling is that of helplessness-hopelessness.

6. *The common cognitive state in suicide is ambivalence.* Freud brought to our unforgettable attention the psychological truth that transcends the surface appearance of neatness of logic by asserting that something can be both A and not A at the same time.

7. *The common perceptual state in suicide is constriction.* I am one who believes that suicide is not best understood as a psychosis, a neurosis, or a character disorder. I believe that suicide is more accurately seen as a more-or-less transient psychological constriction, involving our emotions and intellect.

8. *The common action in suicide is escape or egression.* Egression is a person's intended departure from a region, often a region of distress.

9. *The common interpersonal act in suicide is communication of intention.* One of the most interesting things we have found from the psychological autopsies of unequivocal suicidal deaths done at the Los Angeles Center was that there were clues to the impending lethal event in the vast majority of cases.

10. *The common pattern in suicide is consistent with lifelong long styles of coping.*

Shneidman advises us:

> We must look to previous episodes of disturbance, dark times in that life, to assess the individual's capacity to endure psychological pain. We need to see whether or

not there is a penchant for constriction and dichotomous thinking, a tendency to throw in the towel, for earlier paradigms of escape and egression. Information would be in the details and nuances of how jobs were quit, how spouses were divorced, and how psychological pain was managed.[121]

There are also certain questions we might pose to help get a person out of a constricted suicidal state: Where do you hurt? What is going on? What is it that you feel you have to solve or get out of? Do you have any formed plans to do anything harmful to yourself, and what might those plans be? What would it take to keep you alive? Have you ever before been in a situation in any way similar to this, and what did you do and how was it resolved?[122]

The implications of the 10 commonalities for a suicidal patient in therapy should be fairly obvious: Reduce the pain; remove the blinders; lighten the pressure—all three, even just a little bit. To put it technically (in terms of perturbation and lethality), if you address the individual's perturbation (the sense of things being wrong), that person's lethality (the pressure to get out of it by suicide) will decrease as the perturbation is reduced. That is the goal of therapy with a suicidal person.[123]

Shneidman's colleague Robert Litman tells us: "People commit suicide because they cannot accept their pain, because the pain does not fit in with their concept of themselves, with their personal ideal. So for me, the long-range treatment of chronically suicidal people includes helping them change their self concept so that they can learn to acknowledge that their pain, while unique to

---

[121] Ibid., location 1359.

[122] Ibid., location 1376.

[123] Ibid., location 1382.

them, is not radically different from everyone else's pain, and their personhood is basically pretty much the same as everybody else's personhood."[124]

In his discussion of the ten commonalities Shneidman expresses the opinion that *suicidality springs from psychological assaults "very early in childhood"* and likely *"the pains that drive suicide relate primarily not to the precipitous absence of equanimity or happiness in adulthood, but to the haunting losses of childhood's special joys"* (emphasis added).[125]

David Lester reviews Shneidman's 1970 contention that the formal logic of suicidal reasoning is not as interesting as the actual style of reasoning used by the individual—what Shneidman termed *concludifying*, that is, how the individual reaches conclusions, thinks, reasons, and infers. Lester reviews several other of Shneidman's papers on logic and language and notes that suicidal people do not use language in ordinary ways but that they are inclined to elide ideas and reach faulty conclusions, as in "the only possible conclusion is suicide."[126]

Shneidman in 2001 in *Comprehending Suicide* puts forth many of his conclusions based on a 40-year career studying suicide:

> I believe that suicide is essentially a drama in the mind, where the suicidal drama is almost always driven by psychological pain, the pain of the negative emotions— what I call *Psycheache.* Psycheache is at the dark heart of suicide; no Psycheache, no suicide.
>
> I tentatively believe—guided by my own clinical

---

[124] Litman, quoted by Shneidman, ibid., location 1584.

[125] Ibid., location 1632.

[126] Lester (2004).

experience —that for most practical purposes a majority of suicide cases tend to fall into one of four clusters of frustrated psychological needs. They exhibit themselves in different kinds of psychological pain.

1. *Thwarted love, acceptance, or belonging*—related primarily to the frustrated needs for succor and affiliation.

2. *Fractured control, excessive helplessness, and frustration*—related primarily to the frustrated needs for achievement, autonomy, counteraction, inviolacy, order, and understanding.

3. *Assaulted self-image and avoidance of shame, defeat, humiliation, and disgrace*—related primarily to the frustrated needs for affiliation, autonomy, dependence, shame avoidance, and succor.

4. *Ruptured key relationships and attendant grief and beefiness*— related primarily to the frustrated needs for affiliation and nurturance.[127]

Shneidman here expresses his opinion that all of the demographic, psychiatric, psychoanalytic, or biological studies of past and present are on the archery easel but miss the bull's eye target. *Shneidman believes that reduction of Psycheache created by thwarted psychological needs is the goal.* "For me, today, still, the core data to elicit from a potentially suicidal person are not a family history, a spinal tap assay, a demographic survey, a psychiatric account, a psychodynamic interview, or a self-report of a mental illness, but rather—keeping all of these relevant bits of information in mind—what is directly to the suicidal person's point, namely a full anamnestic response to the two basic questions in clinical suicidology: "Where do you hurt." and "How

---

[127] Shneidman (2001), p. 202.

120

may I help you?"[128]

In *Definition of Suicide* Shneidman summarizes much of his thinking by listing four psychological features that seem to be necessary for a completed suicidal act:

> 1. *acute perturbation*, that is, an increase in the individual's state of general upsetment;
>
> 2. *heightened inimicality*, an increase in self-abnegation, self-hate, shame, guilt, self-blame, and overtly in behaviors which are against one's own best interests;
>
> 3. *a sharp and almost sudden increase of constriction of intellectual focus*, a tunneling of thought processes, a narrowing of the mind's content, a truncating of the capacity to see viable options which would ordinarily occur to the mind; and
>
> 4. *the idea of cessation*, the insight that it is possible to put an end to suffering by stopping the unbearable flow of consciousness. This last is the igniting element that explodes the mixture of the previous three components. In this context, *suicide is understood not as a movement toward death (or cessation) but rather as a flight from intolerable emotion* (emphasis added).[129]

Further, Shneidman holds that the therapist should try to understand not only the hurt that the patient is feeling but, centrally, the "problem" that the individual is trying to solve:

> The focus should not be on "why" suicide has been chosen as the method for solving life's problems, but rather on solving the problems, so that suicide—chosen for whatever reasons—becomes unnecessary (in that the problems are addressed and that the person sees some hope of at least partially satisfying, or redirecting, the

---

[128] Ibid., p. 203.

[129] Shneidman (2014), Kindle version, location 623-628.

urgently felt needs which were central to his suicidal scenario)....

In part, the treatment of suicide is the satisfaction of the unmet needs. One does this not only in the consultation room but also in the real world. This means that one talks to the significant others, contacts social agencies, and is concerned about practical items such as job, rent, and food. The way to save a suicidal person is to cater to that individual's infantile and realistic idiosyncratic needs. The suicidal therapist should, in addition to other roles, act as an existential social worker, a practical person knowledgeable about realistic resources and aware of philosophic issues—a speciality which should be encouraged.... The psychotherapist can focus on feelings, especially such distressing feelings as guilt, shame, fear, anger, thwarted ambition, unrequited love, hopelessness, helplessness, and loneliness. The key is the improvement of the external and internal situations—a J.N.D. (Just Noticeable Difference). This can be accomplished through a variety of methods: ventilation, interpretation, instruction, behavior modification, and realistic manipulation of the world outside the consultation room.[130]

... All this implies—when working with a highly lethal person—a heightened level of therapist-patient interaction during the period of elevated lethality. The therapist needs to work diligently, always giving the suicidal person realistic transfusions of hope until the perturbation intensity subsides enough to reduce the lethality to a tolerable, life-permitting level.[131]

... Another implication for individual therapy: The suicidal individual typically has a (transient) tunneling of perception manifested specifically in a narrowing or shrinking of the options for behavior which occur in his

---

[130] Ibid., location 3308.
[131] Ibid., location 3310.

mind. The options have often been narrowed to only two: To live a certain specific way (with changes on the part of significant others) or to be dead. It follows that the therapist's task is to extend the range of the patient's perceptions, "to widen his blinders," to increase the number of choices, including, of course, the number of viable options.[132]

... The most effective way to reduce elevated lethality is by doing so indirectly; that is, by reducing the elevated perturbation. Reduce the person's anguish, tension, and pain and his level of lethality will concomitantly come down, for it is the elevated perturbation that drives and fuels the elevated lethality.[133]

... With a highly lethal suicidal person the main goal is, of course, to reduce the elevated lethality. The most important rule to follow is that high lethality is reduced by reducing the person's sense of perturbation. One way to do this is by addressing in a practical way those in-the-world things that can be changed if ever so slightly. In a sensible manner, the therapist should be involved with such significant others as the patient's spouse, lover, employer, and government agencies. In these contacts the therapist acts as ombudsman for the patient, promoting his or her interests and welfare. The sub-goal is to reduce the real-life pressures that are sustaining or increasing the patient's sense of perturbation. To repeat: In order effectively to decrease the individual's lethality, one does what is necessary to decrease the individual's perturbation.[134]

... A psychotherapist can try to decrease the elevated perturbation of a highly suicidal person by doing almost everything possible to cater to the infantile idiosyncrasies, the dependency needs, the sense of

---

[132] Ibid., location 3314.

[133] Ibid., location 3345.

[134] Ibid., location 3352.

pressure and futility, and the feelings of hopelessness and helplessness that the individual is experiencing. In order to help a highly lethal person, one should involve others and create activity around the person; do what he or she wants done; and, if that cannot be accomplished, at least move in the direction of the desired goals to some substitute goals that approximate those which have been lost.[135]

... The therapeutic message of this book is not to eschew the ordinary, common-sense gambits of response simply on account of their direct relationship to the nature of suicide itself. Of course, one should use all measures that work (for the therapist and the patient). These include support, psychodynamic interpretation, medication, the involvement of others including social agencies, and so on—all of which serve directly or indirectly to mollify one or more of the common characteristics of suicide.[136]

... A highly suicidal state is characterized by its transient quality, its pervasive ambivalence, and its dyadic nature.[137]

Several other special features in the management of a highly lethal patient can be mentioned. Some of these special therapeutic stratagems or orientations reflect the transient, ambivalent and dyadic aspects of almost all suicidal acts:

1. Monitoring. A continuous (preferably daily) monitoring of the patient's lethality.

2. Consultation. There is almost no instance in a psychotherapist's professional life when consultation with peers is as important as when one is dealing with a

---

[135] Ibid., location 3356.
[136] Ibid., location 3408.
[137] Ibid., location 3410.

highly suicidal patient.

3. Attention to transference. The successful treatment of a highly suicidal person depends heavily on the transference. The therapist can be active, show his concern, increase the frequency of the sessions, invoke the magic of the unique therapist-patient relationship, be less of a tabula rasa, give transfusions of (realistic) hope and nurturance. In a figurative sense I believe that Eros can work wonders against Thanatos.

4. The involvement of significant others. Suicide is often a highly charged dyadic crisis. It follows from this that the therapist, unlike his or her usual practice of dealing almost exclusively with the patient (and even fending off the spouse, lover, parents, or grown children) should consider the advisability of working directly with the significant others.[138]

The Attachment Approach

John Bowlby early in his psychoanalytic career came to believe that attachment in mammals is a biological drive with enormous psychological implications.[139] By the 1970s, his work set off a widespread research project based on his three categories of attachment: secure, insecure clinging, and insecure withdrawing. Later researchers added the category disorganized attachment and all manner of research attention has been focused on understanding these categories and what they mean in human life. In time it was noted that mothers that were able to give coherent and cogent narratives of their own life histories of relationships and memories on the Adult Attachment Inventory tended to produce securely attached toddlers whereas mothers who could

---

[138] Ibid., locations 3415-3421.
[139] Bowlby (1983).

not give clear and cogent accounts of their own emotional and relational histories tended to produce insecure and disorganized attachments in their toddlers. The conclusion became that the process of learning to "mentalize", to put into words, symbols, and gestures emotional and relational experiences in early life allowed for richer and more coherent mental, emotional, and relational development. That is, to the extent a parent is able to mentalize his or her own moment-to-moment emotional and relational experiences, that parent is able to teach their children this same skill and that this mentalization skill is profoundly related to secure attachment and mature emotional and relational development.

Jeremy Holmes, a long-time attachment researcher, turns his attention to the process of mentalizing the suicidal experience. He makes the point that the paradox of mentalization is that being able to think about suicide makes its occurrence less likely and conversely, not being able to mentalize the suicidal choice increases the likelihood of it happening. Holmes has defined mentalization as the ability "to see oneself from the outside, and others from the inside"[140] In the course of growing up we learn to grasp reality with thought that can be fallible. But mentalizing takes perspectivality into account by allowing us to know what we and others do, say, and feel from given points of view.

Holmes sees suicidality as triggered by a collapse in one's attachment network leaving suicide as a viable option. Considered developmentally, such a person has never internalized a secure base that allows a fully secure self in adult life. Without having

---

[140] Holmes (2011), p. 152.

established in infancy reliable mutual affect regulation and mentalization skills with caregivers there is no internal other to turn to for support in despairing moments.

Michel and Valach in discussing the narrative interview with the suicidal patient speak to the importance of attachment in therapy.

> From an attachment perspective, a secure relationship is not merely instrumental in helping the patient to do the work of therapy, it is intrinsic to the benefit: Patients come to experience the painful emotions associated with their suicidal state in the context of an attachment relationship in which they are no longer alone but rather have the sense of their mind being held in mind by the therapist. This experience, in turn, enhances their capacity to mentalize in the midst of emotional states rather than being emotionally overwhelmed in a nonmentalizing suicidal state that is rightly characterized as *cognitive disorientation* (Wenzel N. Beck 2008, p 195). Hence a mentalizing connection is the foundation for treating suicidal patients.[141]

Holmes describes the two types of insecure attachment strategies—deactivating (withdrawing) and hyperactivating (clinging).

> A deactivating individual tends to have had a parent who, although reliable and loving, to a greater or lesser extent rebuffed bids for closeness. By minimizing attachment needs, security is achieved, albeit at the price of partial inhibition of freedom of exploration and emotional expression. Such people tend to have a *dismissing* narrative style clinically and on the AAI [Adult Attachment Inventory]. When interviewed following a

---

[141] Michel & Valach (2011), p. 87.

suicide attempt, they find it hard to describe in any detail the antecedents of the attempt or what they were feeling at the time: "Oh, it's all over now, I don't really want to think about it"; "It just sort of happened, I can't really think why I did it, something must have come over me." They may well fail to show tor follow-up appointments....

The hyperactivating person has had a caregiver who was no less loving but who tended to be inconsistent and forgetful. A good way to get noticed when stressed, and therefore to feel safe, is to escalate attachment needs, to cling, and to make one's presence felt. These individuals have preoccupied narrative styles,... find it hard to tell a coherent story, and tend to leave the interviewer feeling overwhelmed and confused. "Well, it all goes back to when I was 12 and I went on holiday with my friends and felt really left out and fat...." Interviews with such patients may be difficult to terminate, and there may he frequent between-session bids for proximity, telephone calls, and desperate attempts to contact the therapist when another crisis arises.[142]

Holmes outlines two features of disorganized attachment strategies:

First, there is usually difficulty in affect regulation, and second, there are typically problems in mentalizing. In disorganized attachment the psychobiological attachment procedures for dealing with arousal is disrupted. A distressed careseeker has a care provider who is unable to respond effectively and predictably to her infant's distress. Lyons-Ruth and Jacobvitz (2008) characterized the caregiver's ineffective responses as either "frightened/withdrawn" or "intrusive/ self-referential." In the first, the mother seems to "freeze" when the infant is distressed and cannot mobilize her secure-base resources; in the second, the infant's feelings

---

[142] Ibid., pp. 153-154.

are overridden, and the caregiver responds in terms of her own rather the infant's distress. These responses lead, in turn, to bizarre responses on the child's part: dissociated states, repetitive movements, or even mildly self-injurious actions such as head banging.[143]

Holmes sees individuals with insecure and disorganized attachments having difficulties in forming therapeutic alliances and adapting to the rhythms of attachment and separation inherent in the therapeutic process which often leads to untoward countertransference reactions.

> At bottom, mentalizing is a means by which separation and loss are endured, a bridge across the inevitable fractures and ruptures that are intrinsic to intimacy, and it is only on the basis of secure attachment that the insecurity of detachments can he borne. The mental representation of security fades without reinforcement. Absence makes the heart grow fonder for a while, Out of sight, out of mind all too easily takes over. Therapists need to have a sense of how long a suicidal client can survive without contact and to be aware that this may fluctuate depending on circumstances.[144]

Holmes holds that human thought is ultimately relational and that reliable early caregiving that produces secure attachment necessarily involves teaching mentalization skills. *In therapy with individuals presenting insecure and disorganized attachment strategies it becomes the therapist's task to collaborate in mentalizing suicidality.*

> Unmentalizing, the suicidal person knows that death is the answer. He cannot or will not consider other

---

143 Ibid., p. 156.
144 Ibid., p. 162.

possibilities—that this too shall pass. It is the job of a therapy team to build or rebuild the visualizing of a life that could be lived—and/or to keep the patient alive until that becomes feasible. The therapist becomes the other against whom the suicidal person bounces off his suicidal thoughts—a responsive reflexive surface, strong yet sensitive. The patient's denied hope is located temporarily in the therapist—for safe keeping.[145]

---

[145] Ibid., p. 166.

Chapter Five
Other Remarkable People
Who Have Suicided

A. Alvarez

A. Alvarez in *The Savage God: A Study of Suicide* contrasts the philosopher's quick bouts into philosophical chaos with artist's who live in perpetual chaos and agony.

> The Grand Old Men of literature have been both numerous and very grand: Eliot, Joyce, Valery, Pound. Mann, Forster, Frost, Stevens, Ungaretti, Montale, Marianne Moore. Even so, the casualty-rate among the gifted seems out of all proportion, as though the nature of the artistic undertaking itself and the demands it makes had altered radically.... There are. I think, a number of reasons. The first is the continuous, restless urge to experiment, the constant need to change, to innovate, to destroy the accepted styles.... But for the more serious artist experiment has not been a matter of merely tinkering with the machinery. Instead, it has provided a context in which he explores the perennial question, 'What am I?', without benefit of moral, cultural or even technical securities. Since part of his gift is also a weird knack of sensing and expressing the strains of his time in advance of other people, the movement of the modern arts has been, with continual minor diversions, towards a progressively more inward response to a progressively more intolerable sense of disaster. It is as though, by taking to its limits Conrad's dictum, 'In the destructive element immerse', his whole role in society has changed; instead of being a Romantic hero and liberator, he has become a victim, a scapegoat.[146]

---

[146] Alvarez (1971), pp. 259f.

In reviewing *The Savage God*, Edwin Shneidman cites Alvarez as describing

> a whole class of suicides ... who take their own lives not in order to die, but to escape confusion, to clear their heads. They deliberately use suicide to create an unencumbered reality for themselves or to break through the patterns of obsession and necessity which they have unwittingly imposed on their lives. For me, the key word in that chunk of wisdom is the verb *escape*.... Alvarez concludes this beautiful book with an autobiographical Epilogue. Toward the very end of it he says, 'As for suicide: the sociologists and psychologists who talk of it as a disease puzzle me now as much as the Catholics and Muslims who call it the most deadly or mortal sins. It seems to me to be...a terrible but utterly natural reaction to the strained, narrow, unnatural necessities we sometimes create for ourselves.' In sum, this book is a brilliant piece of 20th-century intellectual history seen from the point of view of a historian and a poet who has had a dear and talented friend commit suicide and has himself survived his own serious suicide attempt. There is no other book that combines breath-taking personal experience and scholarship in this way. *Savage God* is an indispensable report by a uniquely prepared person, by fortune and misfortune, and is, in its entirety, a special gift to suicidology.[147]

Virginia Woolf

Kay Jamison in her telling book *Night Falls Fast: Understanding Suicide* gives numerous instances of suicidality with a brief glimpse of Virginia Woolf:

> Virginia Woolf, who suffered through psychotic manias

---

[147] Shneidman (2001), p. 24.

and depressions, wrote in the first of two suicide notes to her husband, "I feel certain that I am going mad again: I feel we can't go through another of those terrible times. And I shan't recover this time. I begin to hear voices, and can't concentrate. So I am doing what seems the best thing to do."... Several days later, she wrote again, and again she blamed her madness for her death:

> Dearest, I want to tell you that you have given me complete happiness. No one could have done more than you have done. Please believe that. But I know that I shall never get over this: and I am wasting your life. It is this madness. Nothing anyone says can persuade me. You can work, and you will be much better without me. You see I can't write this even, which shows I am right. All I want to say is that until this disease came on we were perfectly happy. It was all due to you. No one could have been so good as you have been, from the very first day till now. Everyone knows that. V. Will you destroy all my papers? Woolf then loaded her pockets with heavy stones and walked into the river.[148]

Ralph Barton

American artist Ralph Barton tried to explain this in his suicide note:

> Everyone who has known me and who hears of this will have a different hypothesis to offer to explain why I did it. Practically all of these hypotheses will be dramatic— and completely wrong. Any sane doctor knows that the reasons for suicide are invariably psychopathological. Difficulties in life merely precipitate the event—and the true suicide type manufactures his own difficulties. I have had few real difficulties. I have had, on the contrary,

---

[148] Jamison (1999), Kindle version, location 1171.

an exceptionally glamorous life—as lives go.... And I have had more than my share of affection and appreciation. The most charming, intelligent, and important people I have known have liked me—and the list of my enemies is very flattering to me. I have always had excellent health. But, since my early childhood, I have suffered with a melancholia which, in the past five years, has begun to show definite symptoms of manic-depressive insanity. It has prevented my getting anything like the full value out of my talents, and, for the past three years, has made work a torture to do at all.... It has made it impossible for me to enjoy the simple pleasures of life that seem to get other people through. I have run from wife to wife, from house to house, and from country to country, in a ridiculous effort to escape from myself. In doing so, I am very much afraid that I have spread a good deal of unhappiness among the people who have loved me.[149]

"Barton put on his pajamas and a silk dressing gown, got into bed, opened up his copy of Gray's Anatomy to an illustration of the human heart, and shot himself in the head.... Difficulties in life merely precipitate a suicide, wrote Barton; they do not cause it. There is much evidence to support his belief. But which difficulties are most precipitous? And why? The reversals of fortune, the deaths or divorces that may be blamed for a suicide are the same disasters and disappointments that attend us all. Yet few of us kill ourselves in response."[150] Suicide notes usually give highly personal reasons: "A suicide's excuses are mostly casual. At best they assuage the guilt of the survivors, soothe the tidy-minded and encourage the sociologists in their endless search for convincing categories and theories. They are like a trivial border incident

---

[149] Ibid., location 1172-1183
[150] Ibid.

which triggers off a major war. *The real motives which impel a man to take his own life are elsewhere; they belong to the internal world, devious, contradictory, labyrinthine, and mostly out of sight* (emphasis added)."[151]

Graham Greene

In his memoir *A Sort of Life*, Graham Greene wrote: "miserableness is like a small germ I've had inside me as long as I can remember, and sometimes it starts wriggling."[152] When his miserableness reached intolerable levels he tried a knife, poison and a gun.

Alan Garner

Alan Garner describes his encounter with his manic-depressive condition:

> The next thing I remember is that I was standing in the kitchen, the sunlit kitchen, looking over a green valley with brook and trees; and the light was going out. I could see, but as if through a dark filter. And my solar plexus was numb.... Some contraption, a piece of mechanical junk left by one of the children, told me to pick it up. It was cylindrical and spiky, and had a small crank handle. I turned the handle. It was the guts of a cheap musical box, and it tinkled its few notes over and over again, and I could not stop. With each turn, the light dimmed and the feeling in my solar plexus spread through my body. When it reached my head, I began to cry with terror at the blankness of me, and the blankness of the world.... I was incapable of emotion except that of being incapable

---

151 Ibid., location 1199.
152 Ibid., location 1375.

of emotion. I had no worth. I poisoned the planet.[153]

Hugo Wolf and Robert Lowell

Austrian composer Hugo Wolf described his manic states: "The blood becomes changed into streams of fie; thoughts cascade and ideas leapfrog from topic to topic. Mood is exultant but often laced with a savage and agitated irritability."[154] One is, said Robert Lowell, "tireless, madly sanguine, menaced, and menacing.... Thought is expansive, frictionless, and astonishingly quick; talk is fast and unstoppable; and the senses are acute, engaged, and sharply responsive to the world about them.[155]

Velimir Khlebnikov

"The fluidity of thinking in mania is matched by a seductive, often psychotic sense of the cosmic relatedness of ideas and events. (This dazzle and rush of euphoric mania make it hard for many patients to give it up.)"[156] Russian poet Velimir Khlebnikov claimed to possess

> equations for the stars, equations for voices, equations for thoughts, equations of birth and death. The artist of numbers, he was certain, could draw the universe: Working with number as his charcoal, he unites all previous human knowledge in his art. A single one of his lines provides an immediate lightning like connection between a red corpuscle and Earth, a second precipitates into helium, a third shatters upon the unbending heavens and discovers the satellites of Jupiter. Velocity is infused

---

[153] Ibid., location 1431.
[154] Ibid., location 1456.
[155] Ibid., location 1456.
[156] Ibid., location 1457.

with a new speed, the speed of thought, while the boundaries that separate different areas of knowledge will disappear before the procession of liberated numbers cast like orders into print throughout the whole of Planet Earth.[157]

Edgar Allan Poe

The great American author likewise describes his manic state: "I went to bed & wept through a long, long, hideous night of despair—When the day broke, I arose & endeavored to quiet my mind by a rapid walk in the cold, keen air—but all would not do— the demon tormented me still. I CANNOT live ... until I subdue this fearful agitation, which if continued, will either destroy my life or, drive me hopelessly mad.[158]

Ivor Gurney

Poet and composer Ivor Gurney was hospitalized for shell-shock in World War I and later diagnosed with a schizophrenic condition in which he repeatedly attempted suicide. He wrote to a friend: "This is a good-bye letter, I am afraid of slipping down and becoming a mere wreck—and I know you would rather know me dead than mad.... May God reward you and forgive me." In his poetry he wrote: "There is a dreadful hell within me, And nothing helps. ... I am praying for death, death, death.... There is one who all day wishes to die...has prayed for mercy of Death."[159]

---

[157] Ibid., location 1461.
[158] Ibid., location1569.
[159] Ibid., location 1667.

David Webb

David Webb in his remarkable book, *Thinking About Suicide*, gives a first-person narrative of his long and painful struggle with alcohol and heroin addiction precipitating several suicide attempts. He takes the position that we are story-telling creatures and that by telling our stories in art, writing, song, dance, and theater we can share our deepest pains that make suicidality a crisis of the self "which is a both a perpetrator and a victim of any suicidal act." He believes that (1) calling suicidality a mental illness wrongly pathologises the sacred crisis of the self; (2) a crisis in the self invites self-inquiry that leads to an understanding of one's suicidality, and (3) thinking of suicidality as a crisis of the self corresponds more closely to the lived experience of it.

Webb describes two suicide attempts that followed on two relationship break-ups, but hastens to add that these break-ups were not the cause but rather the triggers that opened up the floodgates to a flow of life-long sadness. The crisis "cannot be adequately described simply in terms of the feelings that are aroused within you when you are actively contemplating suicide. *These feelings have a history, they are old, even ancient* (emphasis added)."

Being a storyteller, Webb uses countless metaphors to describe his experiences. He feels that the metaphor of addiction to suicidality works.

> There is a craving, a deep, urgent craving. And the holding your breath analogy is not bad either. It is like you're gasping for air, unable to breathe. But it is not air that you are gasping for, it is life. And it is not heroin or alcohol that you crave but peace, some freedom from this anguish. When the suicidality is burning hot inside you,

any freedom at all will do. I tried to go to sleep so that I would never wake up—to die by mentally deciding to die…. Eventually the suicide option became the only option. And in time that moment of decision comes….[160]

Hopelessness and helplessness are the two words most frequently associated with suicide…. Hopelessness to me is the 'black hole' of despair, or sometimes a profound feeling of utter emptiness inside. And helplessness is the belief that this empty, black hole is forever, that it could never be otherwise. I have this feeling of being at the bottom of a very deep well, a black hole of meaningless emptiness … a feeling that this helplessness, this agony, will last forever, that nothing but meaningless hopelessness is possible.[161]

Webb came to see his life as divided between his ordinary consciousness of daylight and his hopeless and helpless consciousness of darkness. He felt that his recovery rested on uniting both sides of his consciousness by surrendering to his deep spiritual self. After years of searching and meditation and telling his stories to others he concludes: "Living the divided life is an apt description for the origins of my suicidal crisis of the self. It is also an apt description of my participation in my own oppression, trapped as I was in the divided self of the mind….And what I discovered when I surrendered to the silent embrace of my innermost self is also described well as an end to living a divided life. Finally, my well-being today rests on the decision—indeed the obligation to live divided no more. And *this* is enough.[162]

---

[160] Webb (2010), p. 31.

[161] Ibid., p. 34.

[162] Ibid., p. 173.

Kate Jamison

Jamison begins her first-person narrative of suicidality having drinks years ago with a long-time friend who also suffered from frequent bouts of suicidality. Together they vowed that if either ever seriously contemplated suicide he would call the other and meet for a week at her friend's vacation house on Cape Cod. But then she hastens to add:

> Who were we kidding? Never once, during any of my sustained bouts of suicidal depression, had I been inclined or able to pick up a telephone and ask a friend for help. Not once. It wasn't in me. How could I seriously imagine that I would call Jack, make an airline reservation, get to an airport, rent a car, and find my way out to his house on the Cape? It seemed only slightly less absurd that Jack would go along with the plan, although he, at least, was rich and could get others to handle the practicalities. The more I thought about the arrangement, the more skeptical I became.... It is a tribute to the persuasiveness, reverberating energies and enthusiasms, and infinite capacity for self-deception of two manic temperaments that by the time the dessert soufflés arrived we were utterly convinced that our pact would hold. He would call me; I would call him; we would outmaneuver the black knight and force him from the board.... If it has ever been taken up as an option, however, the black knight has a tendency to remain in play. And so it did. Many years later—Jack had long since married and I had moved to Washington—I received a telephone call from California: Jack had put a gun to his head, said a member of his family. Jack had killed himself....[163]

Jamison, as a clinician, researcher, and teacher had known

---

[163] Jamison (1999), Kindle version, locations 91-102.

personally or consulted on patients who hanged, shot, or asphyxiated themselves; jumped to their deaths from stairwells, buildings, or overpasses; died from poisons, fumes, prescription drugs; or slashed their wrists or cut their throats. She was upset by Jack's suicide but not surprised he hadn't called because "Suicide is not beholden to an evening's promises, nor does it always hearken to plans drawn up in lucid moments and banked in good intentions. ... As a tiger tamer learns about the minds and moves of his cats, and a pilot about the dynamics of the wind and air, I learned about the illness I had and its possible end point. I learned as best I could, and as much as I could, about the moods of death."[164]

Terry Wise[165]

Wise begins her story, *Waking Up: Climbing Through the Darkness*, with the minute the doctor pronounced the diagnosis, "Lou Gehrig's disease" to her husband. That moment changed her life forever. She lived through the agony of nursing him to death without sharing her struggles with anyone and then after a year found herself unable to mourn, to release the extreme sadness and vulnerability of the loss.

> I knew I would be depressed after Pete's death. Yet, progressing through the grieving process had become a fiction. What had begun as an occasional evening of temperately anesthetizing myself had deteriorated into a routine of teasing death's door with a potentially lethal combination of prescription drugs and alcohol.

---

164 *Ibid.*, location 103.

165 Wise, T. L. (2012), Kindle Version

Excessiveness had swallowed up moderation, and the notion of 'just taking the edge off' had become a thing of the past. In the two months following the funeral, I had created a world of Russian roulette where my survival had become based upon the pure luck of passing out just short of an overdose....I was losing the daily battle against the insatiable appetite of depression, and each time I washed down another sedative with the gulp of a martini, the monster of hopelessness took another huge bite out of me. The appealing notion of suicide was perched on the forefront of my mind, blinding my eyes from the possibility of a tolerable future. Although I had no intention of relinquishing my private world of chemical retreat, somehow, through the haze, a barely audible voice hidden deep inside emerged with enough strength for me to recognize that I needed help.[166]

Wise describes five years of tough therapy fighting depression, alcoholism, drug addiction, and suicidality the entire time including one serious overdose, to which her therapist responded:

"There is no more bullshitting, Terry. This is it. Either you make a commitment to this process or you don't. I can't do the work with you if I have to worry about your getting so upset or pissed off that you terminate therapy. Walking out will be a scenario that is reenacted over and over again, and I'm not going to take that chance. I will do whatever I need to do to save your life, and I will remain as available to you as I can, but there are going to be conditions.... Tell me what you need, what you want, so that I have the chance to give it to you, or if I can't, then we have the chance to find a compromise until we both feel more comfortable. I want to show you how to use our relationship to practice this, so that you can have more fulfilling relationships in your life." ...[167]

---

[166] Ibid., locations 768-783.
[167] Ibid., locations 2419-2573.

For the very first time, I made a commitment to therapy without the company of a plan for my death. Embarking on this journey was much like adapting to life after severing my Siamese twin. I now had to feel and think about everything that I had not wanted to matter. With death as the ante, life had forced my hand, laying down its royal flush when I didn't even have a pair. Apparently, I didn't yet know the rules. It was time for me to learn.[168]

Eleven years later, Wise writes: "I no longer have to strain my imagination to feel joy or happiness. I can't say I found the panacea to counter all of life's challenges. Instead, I learned that being emotionally healthy means feeling everything fully and possessing the coping skills to manage any of life's downturns."[169]

After the remarkable success of *Waking Up: Climbing Through the Darkness*, Wise embarked on a national lecture tour to tell her story of finding containment for her infantile dependencies and insecurities in therapy to others who are struggling with suicidality and don't know where to turn.

Edwin Shneidman's "Suicide Autopsy" on Arthur

Shneidman and his colleagues Norman Farberow and Robert Litman developed the "Suicide Autopsy" as a multi-disciplinary research tool for looking into the mysteries of suicide. In this book Shneidman presents an in-depth picture of what such an autopsy looks like. As a metaphor he calls on the 1950 classic Japanese film *Rashomon* by Akira Kurosawa to illustrate how there is no single

---

[168] Ibid., location 2679.

[169] Ibid., location 2680.

way to view the problem of suicide. The father of Arthur writes the forward:

> For centuries, suicide has been shrouded in secrecy. The families of suicide victims have been punished, often relieved of their possessions, sometimes rejected by their communities, the pain of their terrible loss belittled and misunderstood by friends, families, churches, and nations. It has taken courage, decades of understanding, and the steady work of compassionate professionals and everyday survivors to help professionals in therapeutic, spiritual, and community services to realize that the survivors of those who commit suicide must be treated with the same kindness and humanity as those whose loved ones may have died of diseases or been killed in sudden accidents, deaths that bring great sorrow but not the shame that has often surrounded death by self-murder.
>
> Dr. Shneidman's book shatters the secrets, opens the door to forgiveness of Arthur by his family, and to healing of each family member's own wounds. To be able to celebrate the life of our departed loved one and stop the crushing secrecy that can destroy us if we let it, we must go through the pain. Autopsy of a Suicidal Mind is a model of psychological autopsy that should help those who are bereft by a suicide to understand that the secrets are what often kill, and secrets can kill us if we don't let the light of truth and shared feelings enter our journey of grief. For suicide to be transformed from taboo to understanding, we must seek to find why it is so forbidden a subject.[170]

When lecturing at St. Pelagia's Hospital, Arthur's mother, Hannah Zukin, approached Dr. Shneidman with two suicide notes

---

[170] Shneidman (2004), Kindle version, locations 79-119.

from her son with the request that he meet with her to help unravel the meanings of them. It turns out "St. Pelagia was a 15-year-old Christian girl who lived in the fourth century in ancient Turkish Antioch. When threatened with sexual assault by errant soldiers, she eluded them, and "in order to avoid outrage she threw herself to her death from a housetop roof" (Attwater, 1965). She is venerated by Catholics as a maiden martyr. One might say she is the patron saint of suicidology."[171]

Shneidman and his colleagues began their studies by systematically examining hundreds of suicide notes but the results were overall disappointing. However, when the notes could be viewed in the context of life details known to family, friends, and colleagues many meaningful things emerged. This book undertakes a massive project of extended interviews with friends, colleagues, family and then the data is presented to a group of professionals from various fields and each reviewer writes his or her analysis from their perspective. It is rich with detail, but I can only introduce Arthur and highlight a few cogent facts that help the views we are developing here.

> Our patient—call him Arthur—tells us at the very outset of his suicide note what the matter is. It is pain, psychological pain, what I call Psycheache. He hurts living in his own skin. He is wearing an unacceptable painful indwelling psychological catheter that is not adequately fitted, not adequately useful, and not adequately fulfilling. On the whole, he does not feel worthy. He is estranged, and he hurts beyond bearing.

> What do we learn from Arthur's note? What is he trying to tell us? Do we need the interviews to illuminate

---

171 *Ibid.*, location 238.

and provide context to his narrative? I group some phrases that I found noteworthy.

1. A need to control and direct: 'Please do not resuscitate me if alive when found. Please.' 'I want your happiness' (addressed to girlfriend). '[P]lease move on and make a marvelous life for yourself' (addressed to male friend). 'You will survive without me' (addressed to male friend). 'I need you to be happy that I'm out of pain' (addressed to sister).

2. A plea for forgiveness: '[R]emember me and be happy for me. Please be happy for me'; 'I beg you to celebrate for me that I can be free of pain.' '[P]lease understand that this is what I needed for me.'

3. An absolution: 'Those that tried to help me, including my therapist, should not feel that they failed'; 'Don't feel you failed'; 'No one should feel they failed.'

4. Ambivalence and uncertainty: 'I could not be saved I guess'; 'I guess this was inevitable'; 'Right now I am so torn.'

5. Poignant despair: '[H]owever my periods of despair have sadly been there in much greater strength and preponderance.' 'Oh do I wish I was in a simple world where my only needs were food, shelter and clothing, and not some deep spiritual satisfaction.' 'I won't have to struggle with another day.' 'Understand that I was just suffering too much to bear anymore' (addressed to sister). 'I will do it now. I have nothing left.'

6. Remorse and regret: 'I am sorry for leaving you' (addressed to male friend). 'I want so badly to be back with my girlfriend. Why did I ever break up with her then?' 'However, I feel that going back to her just may not be an option at this time.' 'I was not happy and felt there may be a woman out there that could just render me completely content with all of my life.'

7. Being a savior/being saved: 'She is all I feel can save

146

me.' 'I guess I have always dreamt of myself as a savior being someone who would physically drag her off and force me into environments which were good for me and lead me to pleasures in my life.' 'If there is anything above when we are gone, then I will be smiling at you as a close friend when I see you happy in your life. Marry and raise a family' (addressed to girlfriend).

8. Altruism: 'If I go this evening, then I go to spare her more unnecessary pain and to avoid our inevitable cycle of torture.'

9. Lack of pleasure: 'How long can one go without pleasure?' '[A]nd this has taken a great toll on me without anything giving me pleasure in life.'

10. Self-criticism: 'It is the last years that I have managed to slowly ruin my life.' 'I can't hold it together long enough.' '[E]ven if I have been bad at keeping in touch.' 'I can't handle pressure.' 'I lived in isolation. I did not adjust to the school.' 'Somehow I made it through that period.' 'They [the problems] are within me.' 'My life is a tragedy, but it is one that I unfortunately cannot overcome.'[172]

It is notable that all of his friends and family are addressed in the letters *but his mother*. This fact suggests to me that the epicenter of his "Psycheache" centers around his early relation to mother that cannot be remembered except in the role-reversal enactment of neglecting her as she once neglected him—metaphorically forcing her into darkness as she once through neglect forced him.

The overall conclusions are that Arthur may have had some neurological delays or disruptions in infancy and childhood,

---

[172] Ibid., locations 305-339.

as exemplified by severe temper tantrums, running away from home and school, disruptions in the classroom, biting his mother, swinging a baseball bat in the home, and wildly running through the home. His mother described him as dysphoric and anhedonic…. It is unclear how these behavioral problems and poor ability to relate to others interfered with the development of a nurturing relationship between Arthur and his mother. His mother alludes to her own bouts of depression and to feeling overwhelmed as a mother. One has to wonder if she might have been subclinically depressed and 'outmatched' by a 'difficult child.' She describes Arthur as frustrated, frightened, angry, and full of rage.[173]

Shneidman opines that as a man Arthur

seems to have been on a mission—a search—to find an identity, peace of mind, emotional stability, a sense of predictability, and security. Every time he approached it, it eluded him for one reason or another. The high school incident that led to his first suicide attempt was probably due to his realization that the wonderful weekend experience was fleeting and elusive and that he didn't have the wherewithal to ensure that he could create and maintain such good feelings by himself.[174]

… His mother says that it was in medical school that Arthur made a second suicide attempt. He had found another woman to love, but every time they seemed to get close, he ran away (over and over again). Intimacy and vulnerability seemed to scare him. He constantly was searching for people, institutional frameworks, and careers to provide him with the "fix" for his pleasureless world.[175]

… Arthur seemed to lack any psychic reserve. His

---

[173] Ibid., locations 375-381.
[174] Ibid., location 399.
[175] Ibid., location 412.

emotional well was always empty, and he lurched from one fleeting pleasurable episode to another. However, no relationship, no event, and no professional identity lasted very long or long enough. His ex-wife reports that Arthur's times of utmost despair came immediately after happy times.[176]

... He lived for thirteen years beyond his first serious suicide attempt (which required hospitalization). He reports that he never truly gave up the thought or intent to die. My sense is that right up until the end he wanted to be saved but didn't know how to save himself without asking for help—which, ironically, he may have been too ashamed to ask for.

... This is a case of a young man searching for authenticity, identity, and individuation.... Every time he entered into situations that allowed him a taste of these things, they weren't sustainable—either due to circumstances (the high school weekend) or to his inability to adjust to them (his marriage, a long-term commitment to his girlfriend).... I believe that, because he was already struggling with a constant feeling of emotional emptiness and loneliness, the addition of an impending major depressive episode would overwhelm his abilities to function as a physician-lawyer, friend, son, sibling, and lover.[177]

Arthur himself had a fatal interactive flaw: his inability to accept love ("I don't deserve to be happy," "I don't deserve to have a good, attractive woman"). He repeatedly rejected sustaining acts of interpersonal kindness.

The profile depicted by Shneidman suggests the life-long repetition of the "organizing experience" described earlier—

---

[176] Ibid., locations 444-451.
[177] Ibid., locations 451-460.

Arthur's inability to tolerate intimate connections or sustaining social situations due to early traumatic circumstances that left him with "never reach that way again"—certainly the call of darkness.

Drew Sopirak

I would like to conclude this section on personal suicidal careers with the well-known story of Drew Sopirak who to an uproar of applause from his classmates received the outstanding leadership award from his squadron at the U.S. Air Force Academy. But Drew did not return the next day for graduation or receive his officer's commission because only two weeks before he began hearing the voice of God telling him to run naked through the forest and in the aftermath he was hospitalized for severe mental illness. He had been valedictorian of his senior class in Wilmington, Delaware, president of both junior and senior classes, Homecoming King, captain of his sports teams, and star in the senior play. He was accepted both at West Point and the Air Force Academy where he expected he would succeed. In addition to being "drop-dead gorgeous" Drew was well-liked and excelled at everything he tried. Yet eighteen months after the graduation at the Academy, and a long series of hospitalizations for manic-depressive illness and delusional disorders, he went to a gun store where he bought a .38 caliber revolver and shot himself twice in the head. Drew had made a difference. Drew mattered. But consolations were of little help to his friends and family struggling to grasp why he had done such an incomprehensible thing.

His profile suggests again the emergence of the disconnecting "organizing experience" just at the peak moment of success— becoming a commissioned officer and an Air Force pilot.

Chapter Six:

Considering Teen and Child Suicides

Lester has suggested that the suicides of young people often show an imitation effect, much more so than the suicides of older people.[178] We know the effect of peers and teenage idols suiciding. We can surmise the influencing effects of teen suicide chat rooms. We know nationwide teen fascination with suicide and its causes from the best-selling book and now TV series in its second season, *Thirteen Reasons Why* [to commit suicide]. *Thirteen Reasons* has brought suicide into every teen conversation and classroom in the country.

The nineteenth-century sociologist Durkheim studying suicide statistics in the major European countries and declared that the more tightly a society or religion is woven with the fewest possible choices the lower the suicide rate. Conversely, the more freedom of thought and freedom of choice, the greater the possibility that to live or die is among those choices. It is clear that teens today are less tightly structured and therefore experience more choices, including the choice to die.

Jamison raises another possibility:

> A different but not uncommon profile of an adolescent suicide is that of a high-achieving, anxious, or depressed perfectionist. Setbacks or failures, either real or imagined, can sometimes precipitate suicide. It may be difficult to determine the extent of such a child's psychopathology and mental suffering, due to the tendency to try to appear normal, to please others, not to

---

[178] Lester (2004), p. 7.

call attention to oneself. The real reasons for suicide remain fugitive. [179]

This takes me full circle to the Relational Listening approach I am putting forth here that holds that the reasons for suicide and suicide attempts are deeply embedded in the relational templates transferred from the first months and years of life. That is, children and adolescents, like adults, may have many things to say about suicide and its possibilities, but when the threat is serious the reasons go below the level of consciously constructed personal and cultural narratives to the enactment of body-mind and interactional memories transferred into current relationships or relationship situations. All sorts of events in the interpersonal environment can easily trigger these early memories so that they press for enactment. *People at any age simply cannot say what their deep relational reasons are for contemplating suicide because the relational scenarios in danger of being enacted are pre-symbolic, pre-verbal, and pre-narrational—memory experiences that are unformulated and can only be enacted—repeated— in some way.* The mandate for therapy here is clear—set up a safely bounded therapeutic relationship in which these pre-reflective memories can have a place to be safely enacted, narrated, and represented in consciousness and higher levels of relatedness. Let's consider a typical teenage dilemma.

Dead Poets Society

In the 1989 film *Dead Poets Society* English teacher John Keating played by Robin Williams takes us on a journey to explore

---

[179] Jamison (1999), Kindle version, p. 90, location 1244.

the intense conflict between adolescent enthusiasm and idealism and the unbearable, unsympathetic pressure of the adult world.

The film begins in an opening convocation of one of the most prestigious college preparatory schools in the East. As our hero Neil and his friends relax after the ceremony his father comes into the dorm room and harshly forbids him to work on the school annual because he wants him to focus on his studies.

In class Keating, the unorthodox English teacher, works to inspire the boys into reading poetry and a group of them form a secret "dead poets society" that meets in a cave at night not far from the school to read poetry to each other.

Neil discovers there are open tryouts for Midsummer Night's Dream and is wild with ecstasy because he finally has discovered what he wants to do in life – become an actor! His father gets wind of his intention and sternly confronts him and forbids him to continue the play. Keating encourages him to confront his father which he cannot—"I'm trapped." In defiance of his father he is a smashing success in the starring role of Puck.

Enraged his father drags him home and in front of his passive ineffective mother announces that he is being sent to military school tomorrow and to Harvard medical school against his will. He makes an attempt to stand against his father but is forced to back down.

Trapped between knowing his passion and having discovered that he was great at it and his father's rigid demand for conformity a shot in the night announces *the call of darkness.*

Chapter Seven
Suicide Among Older Adults

Highest suicide rates are regularly reported among older adults. The increased rates are presumed to reflect the effects of aging and the threat of illness and dying as well as the emergence of discouragement and depression—helplessness and despair—that often increases with age and aging circumstances. *But there is no reason to suppose that the underlying relational templates from the first two years of life that are being transferred to later-in-life issues are any different than at any other age, though they may be exacerbated by the realities of aging. The danger here for therapeutic listening is to become derailed by narratives regarding the realities or worries regarding health and aging and the losses entailed.*

Relational psychotherapy entails listening for how the primordial relatedness templates—the organizing experience connect-disconnect and the symbiotic experience attachment-abandonment—are being enacted. That is, as we have seen at any other age, the culturally-determined narratives that we use to describe our lives in context seldom represent the realities of the relational templates we are continuing to enact.

Assisted Suicide

In June of 1997, the Supreme Court held that assisted suicide is not a constitutionally protected right and that its legality is left up to the states (Vacco v. Quill and Washington v. Glucksberg). In anticipation of the rulings, in April of 1997, the American Psychological Association (APA) Public Communications Office, in collaboration with the Public Interest Directorate, established a working group to create a briefing paper on mental health issues involved in physician-assisted suicide and other end-of-life decisions.[180]

The Oregon "Death with Dignity" Act states the following:

> An adult who is capable, is a resident of Oregon, and has been determined by the attending physician and consulting physician to be suffering from a terminal disease, and who has voluntarily expressed his or her wish to die, may make a written request for medication for the purpose of ending his or her life in a humane and dignified manner in accordance with ORS 127.800 to 127.897. (Task Force to Improve the Care of Terminally Ill Oregonians, 1998, p. 57)
>
> Other sections of the law are designed to provide safeguards for the practice. For example, the written request must be witnessed by two unrelated persons; there must be a consulting physician; the patient must make an informed decision; the attending or consulting physician can request a referral to a licensed psychologist or psychiatrist if they suspect that a psychiatric condition or depression may be causing impaired decision-making; and family notification is recommended. [181]

The Netherlands has assisted suicide and euthanasia provisions:

> Unlike the United States, both assisted suicide and euthanasia are decriminalized and permissible in the Netherlands under prescribed circumstances. Also, in the Netherlands, there is universal health coverage; the

---

[180] American Psychological Association (2000), p. 40.
[181] Ibid.

population is more homogeneous, with a smaller range of cultural diversity; and family doctors have typically known their patients for long periods of time.... In the past two decades, the Netherlands has moved from considering assisted suicide ... to giving legal sanction to both physician-assisted suicide and euthanasia; from euthanasia for terminally ill patients to euthanasia for those who are chronically ill; from euthanasia for physical illness to euthanasia for psychological distress; and, from voluntary euthanasia to non-voluntary and involuntary euthanasia. [182]

In Switzerland assisted suicide has been legal since 1941 if performed by a non-physician without a vested interest in that individual's death.

The law prohibits doctors, spouses, children, or other such related parties from directly participating in one's death. Many citizens from other countries cross over into Switzerland to end their lives. In 2011, a proposed ban of this practice of "suicide tourism" was rejected by popular vote in the canton of Zürich with a 78% majority. The laws regulating assisted suicide do not limit the practice to the terminally ill, it is only necessary that the person seeking assisted suicide does so while in full possession of their decision-making capacity (and indeed the statistics on assisted suicide show a minority of cases citing depression as relevant illness).[183]

The APA report concludes:

There are numerous opportunities at federal, state, and local levels for psychologists [and other Mental Health Professionals] who are interested in assuming advocacy or policy roles to advance the quality of care at the end of

[182] Ibid., pp. 41 and 43.
[183] Wikipedia, "Suicide in Switzerland."

life. Psychologists can promote a wider societal commitment to caring well for people who are approaching death by working with other health care professionals and managers, researchers, policymakers, funders of health care, and the public at large to improve policy and practice. The goal of widespread quality care at the end of life is attainable, but realization of that goal will require many system-wide changes in attitudes, policies, and actions.[184]

Amour (Love)

Amour is a 2012 French-language film that won major film awards in Europe and garnered five Oscar nominations, including Best Original Screenplay and winning for Best Foreign Language Film. In the opening scene police are breaking down the doors of an apartment of an elderly couple who are both music teachers—because the neighbors have smelled something funny. Both Anne and Georges are found dead.

We are then taken back to a scene from a few months earlier when the tragedy began. While sitting at the breakfast table, Anne experiences a stroke. The symptoms are mild at first but quickly progress. She has surgery, but the procedure goes wrong, leaving her wheelchair-bound and the entire right side of her body paralyzed. Concerned about her prognosis, Anne makes George promise not to send her back to the hospital or a nursing home. One day he comes home to find her in the midst of a failed suicide attempt: she was unable to hoist herself up to jump out of the window she managed to open. She tells Georges that she no longer wishes to live, but Georges will not hear of it.

---

[184] American Psychological Association (2000) op. cit., p 32.

After a second stroke leaves Anne with a form of dementia and unable to communicate orally but for groans and the occasional isolated words, Georges tenderly and patiently cares for her to the best of his ability—feeding, bathing, singing, and reading to her. But finally, on a day when she is particularly agitated and repeatedly making a single bleat, *"Blesse"* (hurt), Georges gently tells her a long story about things that happened in his childhood, then decisively smothers her to death with pillow, finally answering her *call of darkness.*

Georges goes to the market for flowers and prepares her in her best white gown before he takes his overdose. In his delirium he suddenly hears dishes being washed in the kitchen and rises to see her alive and well saying it's time to leave now. She asks him to get her coat. Then he puts on his own coat and they silently walk out together.

Chapter Eight

Other Psychological Approaches to the Prevention of Suicide

There are any number of other psychological views of suicide but I will only survey a few of the more prominent. Quinnett in *Suicide—The Forever Decision* actually captures the spirit of many psychological approaches in welcoming suicidal crises because of what illuminating experiences they can offer. "As I have told many of my suicidal patients, 'A suicide crisis is a terrible thing to waste. What can we learn from what's happening right now that will make your life not just tolerable, but wonderful?[185]

The "Aeschi" Approach

A group of elite suicide researchers and clinicians from all over North America and Europe held their first conference in Aeschi, Switzerland in February 2000 and has continued to meet annually. The initial concern was that subsequent to suicide attempts treated in most hospitals and clinics only a brief evaluation of suicide risk is routinely conducted with little or no follow-up. After careful study and deliberation, the group consensus has become that effective suicide prevention can only be conducted in the context of a viable treatment relationship, a "therapeutic alliance." A number of working principles emerged that led to guidelines for clinicians:

---

[185] Quinnett (2012), Kindle version, location 133.

1. *The clinician's task is to reach, together with the patient, a shared understanding of the patient's suicidality.* The working group holds the view that the goal for the clinician must be to reach, together with the patient, a shared understanding of the patient's suicidality. This goal stands in contrast to a traditional medical approach where the clinician is thought to be the expert in identifying the causes of a pathological behaviour and to make a diagnostic case formulation. It must be made clear, however, that in the working group's understanding a psychiatric diagnosis is an integral part of the assessment interview and must adequately be taken into consideration in the planning of further management of the patient. The active exploration of the mental state, however, should not be placed early in the interview.

2. *The clinician should be aware that most suicidal patients suffer from a state of mental pain or anguish and a total loss of self-respect.* Patients therefore are very vulnerable and have a tendency to withdraw. Experience suggests, however, that after a suicide attempt there is a "window" in which patients can be reached. Patients at this moment are open to talk about their emotional and cognitive experiences related to the suicidal crisis, particularly if the clinician is able to explore the intrasubjective meaning of the act with the patient.

3. *The interviewer's attitude should be non-judgmental and supportive.* For this the clinician must be open to listen to the patient. Only the patient can be the expert of his or her own individual experiences. Furthermore, the first encounter with a mental health professional determines patient compliance to future therapy. An open non-pejorative approach is essential to support patients in reconsidering their goals.

4. _The interview should start with the patient's self-narrative._ A suicidal crisis is not just determined by the present, it has a history. Suicide and attempted suicide are inherently related to biographical, or life career aspects and should be understood in this context. Therefore, the interview should start with the patient's self-narrative ("I should like you to tell me, in your own words, what is behind the suicide attempt...."). Explaining an action, and making understood to another person what made the individual do it puts a suicidal crisis into perspective and can be instrumental in re-establishing the individual's sense of mastery.

5. _The ultimate goal must be to engage the patient in a therapeutic relationship._ The meaningful discourse with another person can be the turning point for the patient in that life-oriented goals are re-established. This requires the clinician's ability to empathize with the patient's inner experience and to understand the logic of the suicidal urge. An interview in which the patient and the interviewer jointly look at the meaning of the suicidal urge sets the scene for the dealing with related life-career or identity themes. The plan of a therapy is so to speak laid out.

6. We need new models to conceptualize suicidal behaviour that provide a frame for the patient and clinician to reach a shared understanding of the patient's suicidality. An approach that does not see patients as objects displaying pathology but as individuals that have their good reasons to perform an act of self-harm will help to strengthen the rapport. The most common motive is to escape from an unbearable state of mind (or the self). A theoretical model that understands suicide actions as goal directed and related to life-career aspects may prove to be particularly useful in clinical practice. The group strongly feels that purely reductionist, quantitative research alone cannot fully reveal the complex processes that give rise to a person's suicidal behaviour. While quantitative research has helped guide clinical interventions, there is an increasing need for qualitative research focusing on the patients' own internal suicidal processes as well as on interactive processes with professional helpers. We can expect that such research will add new dimensions to the existing knowledge of the suicidal process.[186]

A remarkable collection of papers offering various approaches to suicide prevention that are compatible with the Aeschi recommendations has been edited by Swiss psychiatrist Konrad Michel and American psychologist David Jobes and published by the American Psychological Association, *Building a Therapeutic Alliance with the Suicidal Patient* (2011). A number of ideas and approaches collected in this set of papers appear in the following text.

In the Aeschi spirit, Jobes and Ballard (2011) see suicide as an interpersonal act, that is, much of suicidal behavior revolves around struggles with relational issues and communication of intention.

> ... suicidal acts and communications are deeply rooted within interpersonal-relational-social struggles, and each is clearly designed to reveal a range of important intentions that are inextricably wrapped within their suicidal acts.... It is thus plain that many suicidal states are fundamentally defined and connected to either the existence or absence of certain key relationships.[187]
>
> When two people meet in a therapeutic context, they need a common ground to establish some kind of meaningful interaction ... suicidal actions become intelligible only through a person's narrative. When

---

[186] http://www.aeschiconference.unibe.ch/Guidelines_for_clinicians.html (retrieved January 1, 2018).

[187] Jobes & Ballard (2011), p. 52.

patients are actively encouraged to tell the story behind a suicide attempt, and when the interviewer is open to listen, patients are well able to tell their story. They want to interpret what happened themselves and create a picture of how they want the health professional to understand their action.... By joining the patient in the understanding of the suicidal act in a biographical context, the therapist has the unique experience of gaining an insider's view of the patient's suicidality.[188]

The Dialectical Behavior Therapy (DBT) Approach

Marsha Linehan developed Dialectical Behavior Therapy to work with suicidality and the population of patients diagnosed "borderline personality disorder." DBT is a manualized approach to treatment with things for the therapist to do and not do in treatment. She established clearly that this population of character disorders required long-term treatment—a year or more—with a minimum of one individual and one group session weekly with homework in between and greater frequency when needed. DBT uses treatment strategies from behavioral, cognitive, and supportive therapies. It is known that there is a high rate of suicides in this population and Linehan has set up a set of clear protocols on how therapists are to handle suicidality.[189] Williams describes the approach:

A behavioural/problem-solving component focuses on enhancing capability, generating alternative ways of coping, clarifying and managing contingencies, all with the emphasis on the 'here and now'. The 'dialectical' aspect lies in its emphasis on balancing *acceptance* of

---

188 Ibid., p. 77.
189 Linehan (1991).

(seeing clearly) the stresses that exist in the environment on the one hand with the need to *change* them on the other. The theme is encouraging clients to really grasp things, to understand them deeply as they are and to step back from them temporarily in order to see what might be changed. [190]

Jamison reports on Linehan's review of twenty controlled clinical trials utilizing different forms of psychotherapy with patients at high risk of suicide. "In most studies, the patients were selected on the basis of having made at least one suicide attempt. The psychotherapeutic interventions that seemed to be most effective, particularly in patients with borderline personality disorder, sharply focus on changing specific suicidal behaviors and thoughts. These therapies, especially those that are based on identifying and modifying maladaptive behaviors and thinking, appear to work reasonably well in decreasing deliberate self-harm."[191] "The therapies that appear most promising are those that make the links between thoughts, feelings and behaviors more explicit ... [DBT] involves an 'exhaustive description of the moment-to moment chain of environmental and behavioural events that preceded the suicidal behaviour.... Alternative solutions that the individual could have used are explored, behavioural deficits as well as factors that interfere with more adaptive solutions are examined, and remedial procedures are applied if necessary.' [... All this] is helped by training in mindfulness skills."[192]

---

[190] Williams (2014), p. 211.
[191] Jamison (1999), Kindle version, p. 255.
[192] Williams (2014) op. cit., p. 211.

Linehan describes the task of the therapist in responding to suicidal behavior as twofold:

(1) responding actively enough to block the patient from actually killing or seriously harming herself; and (2) responding in a fashion that reduces the probability of subsequent suicidal behavior.... Complicating all of this are the fears almost all therapists have of being held responsible for a patient's death if a false step is taken or a mistake made....There are *only* three arbitrary rules in DBT concerning suicidal behavior....First, parasuicidal acts and suicide crisis behaviors are always analyzed in depth; they are never ignored. Second, a patient who engages in parasuicidal acts cannot call her therapist for 24 hours following the act, except in a medical emergency where she needs the therapist to save her life. Even then, the patient should call emergency services and not the therapist. Third, potentially lethal patients are not given lethal drugs....

Suicidal behavior strategies should be used in at least four situations: (1) The patient reports previous suicidal behavior to her individual primary therapist...; (2) the patient threatens imminent suicide or parasuicide to her primary therapist; (3) the patient engages in parasuicide while contact with her primary therapist, or contacts him or her immediately.... (4) When the patient is in crisis and also suicidal, the crisis strategies just described should be integrated with the steps summarized in detail in a table of Suicidal Behavior Strategies Checklist.[193]

Linehan points out as Bonger (1991) and others have suggested, it is naive for the clinician not to consider appropriate clinical and legal issues when treating high-risk populations. Bongar suggests a number of clinical and legal risk management

---

[193] Linehan (1991), op. cit., pp. 467ff.

strategies that are incorporated into DBT. These include the following:

1. *Self-assessment of technical and personal competence* to treat suicidal behaviors is essential. A therapist should refer a patient or obtain supervision and additional training if his or her competence is not sufficient.

2. *Meticulous and timely documentation* is required. The therapist should keep thorough records of suicide risk assessments; analyses of the risks and benefits of various treatment plans; treatment decisions and their rationales (including decisions not to hospitalize a patient or not to take other precautions); consultations obtained and advice received; communications with the patient and with others about treatment plans and associated risks; and informed consents obtained. The general rule of thumb here is "What isn't written didn't happen."

3. *Previous medical and psychotherapy records* should be obtained for each patient, especially as these relate to treatment for suicidal behaviors.

4. *Involving the family,* and if necessary the patient's support system (with the permission of the patient), in management and treatment of suicidal risk; informing family members of risks and benefits of proposed treatment versus alternative treatments; and actively seeking the family's support for keeping the patient engaged in treatment can be very useful.

5. *Consultation with other professionals* about general management and risk assessment is a part of standard

treatment of suicidal behaviors. The nonmedical clinician should consult specifically with medical colleagues about the advisability of using medication or the need for additional medical evaluation.

6. *Postvention* following a patient's suicide–including addressing personal and legal issues, counseling with other staff members involved in the patient's care, and meeting and working with family and friends can be extremely difficult. Consultation with a knowledgeable colleague about postvention steps, including legal consultations, is strongly recommended by many.[194]

The Transference-Focused Psychotherapy Approach

A group of researchers and clinicians led by Otto Kernberg at the Personality Disorders Institute at Cornell University has developed a manualized and empirically validated psychoanalytic psychotherapy derived from various modified psychoanalytic approaches that seeks to address people whose personality development is not suitable for standard psychoanalysis.[195]

> The specific objective of TFP is the modification of the personality structure of patients with severe personality disorders, particularly borderline personality disorder, but also narcissistic, paranoid, schizoid and schizotypal personality disorders....TFP is focused not only on reducing the symptoms typically seen in severe personality disorders, such as chronic suicidal behavior, antisocial behavior, substance abuse, and eating

---

[194] Bongar (1991).

[195] Kernberg (2016).

disorders...but also has the ambitious goal of modifying the personality structure of the patient sufficiently to meaningfully improve functioning in the arenas of work, studies and profession, and intimate relations, such that the individual develops a fuller capacity to integrate emotional commitment, sexual freedom, and tenderness. Such integration leads to improvements in the capacity for genuine friendships as well as investment in creative and cultural pursuits (Yeomans et al., 2015).

The main strategy in the treatment of patients with borderline personality organization consists in the facilitation of the (re)activation of split-off internalized object relations of contrasting persecutory and idealized natures that are then observed and interpreted in the transference. TFP is carried out in face-to-face sessions, with a minimum of two and usually not more than three sessions a week. The patient is instructed to carry out free association while the therapist restricts his or her role to careful listening and observation of the activation of regressive, split-off relations in the transference and to help identify them and interpret their segregation in the light of these patients' enormous difficulty in reflecting on their own behavior and often on the maladaptive, turbulent interpersonal interactions in which they find themselves. The interpretation of these split-off object relations is based upon the assumption that each reflects a dyadic unit comprised of a self-representation, an object representation, and a dominant affect linking them, and that the activation of these dyadic relationships determines the patient's perception of the therapist. Not infrequently, rapid role reversals of idealized and persecutory aspects appear in the transference providing the clinician with a vital window into the patient's internal world of object relations. Thus, the patient may identify with a primitive self-representation while projecting a corresponding object representation onto the therapist, while, ten minutes later, for example, the patient identifies with the object representation while projecting the self-representation onto the therapist.[196]

The main techniques are essentially the same as psychoanalysis, i.e., interpretation, transference-countertransference analysis and neutrality. A treatment contract is established, a priority of themes is set each session, the differences in points of view on reality between therapist and patient, and regulating the intensity of emotional involvement. TFP assumes that it is always *a relationship* that is activated and projected in transference and countertransference. Interpretations seek to address conscious and preconscious experiences of the patient that are in harmony with the person's sense of subjectivity.

The increased attention to the patient's conflicts in external reality does not have the predominant objective of raising the patient's mentalization process regarding these external circumstances, but of exploring the transferential significance of the dissociation of potentially dangerous developments in the patient's life from the treatment situation. Our efforts are not oriented to directly influence the patient's behavior through better understanding his motivation and those of others in such external situations, but acquire an awareness of the transferential significance of keeping potential self-destructive development from potential therapeutic understanding and help.[197]

TFP attempts to bridge the paradox between entering each session "without memory or desire" while at the same time

---

196 Kernberg, pp. 386f.
197 Ibid., p. 387

staying tuned in to the patient's realistic life situation in the areas of: (1) studies, work or profession; (2) love and sexuality; (3) family and social life; and (4) personal creativity. The work is done in two to three times weekly appointments. With regard to self-destructive behaviors Kernberg enunciates a general principle: "the therapist should maintain a high degree of alertness and 'impatience' with a patient's self-induced threats to his wellbeing within each hour, while remaining patient over the long term in analyzing self-destructive and other major characterological problems of the patient. Patience over the long term and 'impatience' in each session are complementary tactical approaches."[198]

There is considerable concern with contract breaches and "second chances," an issue especially important in suicidal behaviors. One of the standard rules is that if suicidal activities occur the patient is not to contact the therapist for 24 hours except for life-saving emergencies, but rather find ways of waiting until the next session or go to an emergency room. Breaking this relational contract is seen as destroying the therapeutic relationship and is cause for immediate termination. However, if appropriate, a "second chance" can be negotiated in light of the transference and countertransference variables operating and interpreted.

> It may be difficult for the therapist to consistently hold in mind the urgency of this issue, in spite of its coloring all other aspects of the treatment developments, and may in fact, represent a chronic, yet acute, severe risk of interruption of the treatment, that is, a 'highest priority'

---

[198] Ibid., p. 394

issue co-determining the 'selected fact' in any session. The patient may not refer again to the contract breach, and present other issues as affectively dominant, distracting the therapist's attention from a potential breach in preparation. Yet, remaining vigilant to this risk may be extremely helpful to the patient and prevent a failed treatment. Concretely, this implies linking the potential threat to the continuation of the therapy when it appears that transference developments are consonant with this threat, interpreting the implicit acting out of destructive transference impulses by repetition of the specific contract breach. Particularly with chronically suicidal tendencies this concern needs to be maintained through all sessions until it becomes clear in the patient's material that now suicide has become a completely irrelevant issue, no longer meaningful in the context of patient's present functioning. In short, the shifting transference implications of the same threat of a second, treatment ending contract breach need to be included, whenever appropriate, in the interpretive interventions of the therapist. When a patient convincingly tells a therapist that he should stop talking about suicidal threats that have not been on the patient's mind for months, and that he no longer can imagine would be able to control him, the therapist may stop bringing up the subject again and again in different transferential contexts! However, as a safety measure, the therapist needs to maintain in mind the constant presence of the risk of temptations to end the treatment when a 'second chance' period evolves in the treatment.[199]

Kernberg closes his discussion with:

In the United States, given the litigious nature of the American culture, it would be absolutely essential to set down a written record of the full communication of these

---

[199] Ibid., p. 401

risks and the acceptance of these risks by the family. Sometimes, even a letter of understanding with family and patient may be indispensable. Behind these arrangements, then, lies the need to assure the security of the therapist in carrying out the treatment. The security of the therapist–physical, emotional, social, and legal, and the protection of his property and personal life–are essential preconditions for the possibility of treating patients with severe personality disorders. If the therapist cannot control any of these boundaries and protect them from severe patient acting out, the treatment may not be viable, and it may be preferable not to engage in it or to stop it. One other major advantage of the treatment procedure and corresponding contract arrangements is their effectiveness in reducing the secondary gain of the symptom, the prevention of the symptoms from becoming a powerful mechanism of omnipotent control and transference acting out.[200]

The Interpersonal Theory of Suicide Approach

A group of researchers and clinicians let by Thomas Joiner has devised an Interpersonal approach which holds that the only people capable of death by suicide are those who have experienced enough past pain to have habituated to the fear and pain of self-injury sufficiently so that the instinct of self-preservation can be overcome. Any strong fear and pain experiences can produce the *acquired capability* to enact self-death. But a second requirement is the *desire* to end their lives. So the question becomes who are the people with suicidal desire? The theory answers: those that have experienced two

---

[200] Ibid., p. 402

interpersonally states of mind, *perceived burdensomeness* and *failed belongingness*. The many ways these predisposing factors may operate in a person's life are detailed by Joiner and his colleagues. "The three factors previously noted—acquired capability, perceived burdensomeness, and failed belongingness—are proposed as answers to the questions of who can die by suicide and who would want to.... Those who both can and want to are at highest risk of serious suicide attempt or lethal self-injury."[201]

An interesting implication of this approach is that those whose jobs entail working with fear, pain, and injury are among those who are habituated vicariously to physical pain and therefore may be more vulnerable. Likewise past suicide attempts may have had an habituating effect. The interpersonal theory suggests that clinicians should be assessing risks in two domains: desire and capability. This will necessarily include the current and long-term risks.

To assess thwarted belongingness, therapists can ask clients the following questions: "Do you feel connected to other people?"; "Do you live alone?"; and "Do you have someone you can call when you're feeling badly?" According to the theory, therapists should he particularly alarmed for clients for whom caring, meaningful connections to others, are completely absent. To assess perceived burdensomeness, therapists can pose the following question: "Sometimes people think, 'The people in my life would be better off if I was gone.' Do you think that?" [202]

---

[201] Joiner et al. (2009), p. 6.
[202] Ibid., p. 57.

The book contains a number of very useful forms and tools. One that asks a series of penetrating questions is the Interpersonal Needs Questionnaire and another is the Acquired Capability Questionnaire. As exhibits the authors offer the Theory-based Assessment Form, The Commitment to Treatment Contract, A Crisis Card that reminds people of how they have decided to handle suicidal crises, A Suicidal Check List for Young Adults and Adolescents, and other clinically useful forms and assessments.

One of the key contributors to the Interpersonal Theory is David Rudd. He believes that the first therapeutic task is developing a relationship.

Establishing a relationship in the initial evaluation with a suicidal patient can be hampered by the severe nature of the psychopathology presented. It is important to keep the following in mind:

1. The patients you see are likely to have difficulty in interpersonal situations. More specifically, it is likely that they have interpersonal skill deficits.

2. Remember the patients you are seeing are likely at their worst because they are actively suicidal. Expect your patients to have trouble with communication. Expect your patients to need reassurance and comfort. It is important for the clinician to recognize that patients in acute suicidal crisis feel powerless and out of control already.

3. Anticipate the possibility of being provoked by suicidal patients, for those with chronic suicidal problems, provocative and undercontrolled behavior is oftentimes routine. Responding to provocation is straightforward.

4. Acknowledge the patient's upset in the context of the current crisis and redirect the patient to the task at hand, emphasizing the collaborative nature of the evaluation process.

5. Recognize that in completing the initial assessment process you are laying the groundwork for ongoing care, regardless of whether or not that care is provided by you. Evaluations and assessments are psychotherapeutic exchanges; there is simply no way around this reality.

6. Conceptualize the therapeutic relationship and alliance as part of the assessment and management process.

7. Use clear, unambiguous language. Do not leave any room for misinterpretation when talking about the issue of suicide.

8. Maintain good eye contact when asking difficult questions. Patients understand the subtleties of interpersonal exchanges, such as markers of discomfort and impatience. The lack of eye contact is an easy one to recognize.

9. From time to time, provide historical and developmental context for the current relationship. The most effective way to do this is to draw parallels between the patient's developmental history, recurrent interpersonal problems, and how these patterns might emerge in the therapeutic relationship.

10. When the opportunity emerges, ask specific questions about problems the patient has had during previous treatment.

11. Make the therapy relationship a routine and consistent item on the treatment agenda if the patient continues beyond the initial evaluation (e.g., designate a few minutes at the end of every other session to talk about it). It is important to place the therapeutic relationship in proper perspective.[203]

The book by Joiner and his colleagues, *The Interpersonal Theory of Suicide* is overall very readable, straightforward and sensible with many helpful forms, a useful addition to a clinician's library.

The Cognitive Approach

Rudd and Brown offer a Cognitive Theory of Suicide.

> Individual vulnerability during an acute suicidal state is pervasive. Targeting symptom recovery through crisis management and skill building not only improves the patient's ability to more fully participate in care but also results in simultaneous improvements in self-esteem, efficacy, and the overall quality of the interpersonal exchange because the patient sees the therapist as both credible and effective.... Patients need a simple and understandable model for how to think about the therapeutic relationship in treatment.[204]

Rudd and Joiner (1997) offer the *Therapeutic Belief System* (TBS) as a cognitive alternative to traditional transference-countertransference models.

> The core elements of the TBS include beliefs about the three critical elements of treatment: the patient's role in

---

[203] Rudd (2006), pp 24-25.
[204] Rudd & Brown (2011), p. 178.

treatment (self), the clinician's role, and the treatment process itself. What is important for practicing clinicians to keep in mind is the importance of translating tacit beliefs to active ones, helping the patient recognize how beliefs across these three domains can either facilitate recovery or undermine care. For example, if the patient believes he or she should have a passive role in care, it is likely this belief will emerge in limited use of the crisis-response plan and related self-management efforts. It is also likely that such a belief would he related to a range of fantasy-based beliefs about the role of the therapist (e.g., "You can read my mind," "You're supposed to just know what's going on with me," "If you really cared, you would know"). The net outcome would be difficulty not only in treatment progress but also in the relationship itself. Clearly, there will be a relationship across the three domains. That relationship is most evident in beliefs about treatment itself (e.g., "Treatment is hopeless," "Treatment is going nowhere fast")....

The TBS offers a simple and straightforward approach to monitoring the therapeutic relationship in cognitive therapy. I recommend that it become a routine part of the treatment agenda. At the beginning of care, it is important to dedicate time to discussing the patient's beliefs about his or her role in treatment, the therapist's role, as well as the treatment process in general. This can include questions about expectations regarding care, as well as a discussion of previous treatment experiences, including successes and, most important, perceived failures.... Effective treatment for suicidality is all about the development, facilitation, and maintenance of hope. In addition, the facilitation of hope starts with an approach that helps set the foundation for a strong therapeutic relationship.[205]

---

[205] Ibid., p. 179

Mindfulness-Based Cognitive Therapy Approach

Another cognitive approach has been developed by a team of researchers and clinicians led by Mark Williams at Oxford. Not unlike other cognitive therapies MBCT targets processes that keep people in "mind-lock"—an inability to recognize and disengage from mind states. It seeks to

> give patients the ability to see thoughts as mental events rather than facts, to decouple the occurrence of negative thoughts from the responses they would usually elicit and, eventually, to change their implicit meaning. However, while Cognitive Therapy maintains a strong focus on the *content* of thoughts and the reevaluation of their meaning, the main aim in MBCT is to teach patients to take a different perspective on thinking itself. By consistently practising bringing awareness to present-moment experience, participants shift into a mode of functioning that is incompatible with the self-focused and analytical cognitive processes that perpetuate the sense of being trapped in depression. Segal, Williams and Teasdale describe this as a change from a 'driven-doing' mode, in which the main focus is on a desperate attempt to reduce the gap between 'how I feel now' and ideas of 'how I should be feeling' by ruminating or avoidance, to a mode of 'being', in which the individual is in immediate and intimate contact with present-moment experience, whatever that might be.[206]
>
> The transformation seems to come when participants, having learned first to focus their attention so it is not hijacked all the time by emotion, then learn to 'decentre' as a means of becoming aware of their thoughts, feelings and bodily sensations. Gradually, they discover a way to bring a sense of perspective and a spirit of 'allowing', kindness and compassion to their

---

[206] Williams (1997/2014), p. 224.

inner experience of suffering. Negative thoughts are viewed as mental events that can be seen clearly in the mental landscape, then let go of. This increased awareness reduces the automatic tendency to get entangled in habitual ruminative thinking. It ultimately leads to a profound shift towards seeing things more clearly, moment by moment. Across the eight sessions of MBCT different guided meditation practices--including an eating meditation, 'body scan', yoga stretches, walking meditation and sitting meditations--are introduced to participants. Towards the end of the treatment participants are encouraged to develop a home practice which fits their needs and which can be maintained in the longer term.[207]

Details of the program can be found in *Mindfulness and the Transformation of Despair: Working with People at Risk of Suicide* (New York: Guilford Press, 2015).

The Collaborative Assessment and Management of Suicidality (CAMS) Approach

The CAMS approach is to form a strong treatment alliance by means of a collaborative assessment of the patient's subjectivity with regards to suicidal experience and suicidal risk and then to set up a co-constructed treatment plan designed to lower risks and avoid an inpatient setting.

In terms of procedures, the CAMS approach employs a multipurpose clinical tool called the Suicide Status Form. The SSF is a seven-page clinical tool that functions in four distinct ways:

1. the initial assessment and documentation of suicidal risk,

---

[207] Ibid., pp. 224f.

2. the initial development and documentation of a suicide-specific treatment plan,

3. the tracking and documentation of ongoing suicidal risk assessment and updates of the treatment plan, and

4. the ultimate accounting and documentation of clinical outcomes.[208]

Jobes et al. (in press) recently clarified and further elucidated CAMS:

> CAMS is a clinical approach with suicidal patients that embraces an overall therapeutic philosophy and employs the use of a particular of procedures that continuously emphasize patient-clinician collaboration and an on-going clinical focus on suicidality. In other words, CAMS is a therapeutic *framework* that mental health clinicians can use until their patients' suicidal thoughts and behaviors resolve. After the index assessment at the initial intake, resolution of suicidality is operationally achieved through clinical judgment and the monitoring of on-going SSF ratings to determine when three consecutive appointments have occurred wherein the patient no longer has any suicidal thoughts, feelings, or behaviors. Previous research and clinical experience has shown that clinical resolution of suicidality using CAMS may occur in as few as 4 sessions but may take up to 19 sessions; the average number of sessions to resolution in CAMS is 8-12 meetings.
>
> Adherence to CAMS requires a thorough suicide risk assessment and problem-focused interventions that are specifically designed to decrease suicide risk. Both assessment and intervention require a collaborative approach demonstrated by, but not limited to: (a)

---

[208] Jobes et al. (2011), pp. 206-208.

empathy with the suicidal wish; (b) clarification of the CAMS agenda, particularly in first session but also any time it is needed; and (c) all assessments and interventions are designed and modified interactively with equal input from both parties. Both assessment and intervention also require maintaining continuous attention on directly reducing suicidality.[209]

Psychiatric Approaches

There is much controversy around the question of the relationship of suicidality to psychiatric diagnosis. Some hold that a person who actually takes his/her life is psychotic at the time. Other opinions hold that suicide attempts and parasuicidal behaviors are always associated with character disorder manipulations. Many hold that there are many rational reasons why a person might contemplate or attempt suicide and that being suicidal during trying times of life is normal. Thomas Joiner and his colleagues point out that psychiatric diagnoses are often associated with suicide so that clinicians need to be alert to what they call the big five: major depressive disorder, bipolar disorder, anorexia nervosa, schizophrenia, and borderline personality disorder. Although substance dependence and other character disorders may also increase suicide risk.[210]

Before the publication of this paper the distribution of suicide among the different diagnostic groups was little more than conjecture. Indeed, it was still possible to presume, as many writers did, that "normal" individuals without mental illnesses committed suicide.

---

[209] Ibid.

[210] Joiner et al. (2009), p. 21.

However, prior to the St. Louis study the distribution of diagnoses associated with suicidality was mostly conjecture. Robins and colleagues investigated all the suicides that took place in St. Louis over the course of a year and "discovered something remarkable—that 98 percent of them were clinically ill, and that 94 percent had a major psychiatric illness (none were merely "neurotic"). They established that 68 percent of the total group suffered from either manic depressive disease or chronic alcoholism. What they found was substantially validated by two later studies (Dorpat & Ripley 1960; Barraclough et al. 1974)."[211]

---

[211] Robins et al. (1996), p. 143.

Chapter Nine
A Clinical Case:
'Night, Mother by Sarah Turner-Miller[212]

Hedges' Introduction

Therapists frequently do not have the opportunity to see and to enjoy the fruits of their work. Practical issues as well as significant transference-countertransference issues may crop up to cut short the therapeutic relationship, leaving the listener bewildered, "holding the bag."

Yet as often happens, perhaps years later, the listener by chance encounters news that attests to the powerful and beneficial effect on the person's life that the emergence of transference into the full light of day has had.

Therapists tend to feel more secure when the transference manifestations are clarified (and "resolved") in the "working through" phase. But this was not Freud's criterion for cure. He believed that the mere establishment of the "transference neurosis" within consciousness was sufficient to merit the term *cure.*[213]

We do not have sufficient experience with the "transference symbiosis" to be so confident about a favorable outcome from the mere conscious experiencing of transference as Freud was about "transference neurosis," but I have the impression that in many instances of what the listener may consider "premature

---

[212] This is an adaptation of the full case study in Hedges (1996).

[213] For elaboration of Freud's position, see Hedges (1983), pp. 36-41.

185

termination," the speaker's way of life has undergone transformations of considerable proportions. French psychoanalyst Andre Green assures us that the central function of psychoanalytic therapy is "representation" in word or deed.[214]

Perhaps the reader will be willing to speculate about what effects the following therapeutic relationship had on this analytic speaker who tells her story in terms of a familiar film plot. The following vignette spans only one year but is intense, vivid, dangerous, and deeply disturbing to the therapist. Freud teaches that it is often necessary for people to find some way of turning passive trauma into active victory. This seems to be the nature of this patient's use of therapy and her therapist.

Turner-Miller:

This case vignette is written from my process notes as they occurred and from the patient's unsolicited letters and artwork presented to me, as well as dreams and other material from our sessions.

Notes from First Session (September)

Dark trouble. This particular referral source wouldn't send me such a nightmare; wouldn't even know a person like this. Listen to my naive, snob Pollyanna. Maybe I'm having a rough day. Impressions are unusually strong, so I'll jot them down. Maggie is a middle-aged woman, groomed but untidy. She has a worn, thrift-store look in a hand-crocheted sweater made of hard acrylic yarn. She doesn't hang together. Her body lacks structure, like jelly. Her

---

[214] Personal communication.

large eyes not only stared, but looked through me so hard I felt very uncomfortable. She clutched her purse and told me I was her last stop! She doesn't mean today, either. I feel like I am an innocent person in the middle of some kind of dangerous conspiracy. This sounds so far out. I don't like how I feel. Perhaps next time will be different. Maybe I shouldn't take her on. I already told her I would and gave her another appointment. I feel compelled. Why? I saw and felt the desperation—there's my soft place again, the fundamental therapist functioning that is part of my own personal identity.

October Notes

Those eyes always look frightened, yet aggressive; like a caged animal cornered and ready for more trauma. Maggie tells me she cannot sleep and feels very agitated. She feels ugly, that she doesn't belong on earth, that others are better; that she is a child of God, but only a figment of God's imagination. "I feel like I don't exist." She feels set apart, more intelligent, and superior, even though others are experienced as "better" than she.

She related her early history: she was adopted at 4 months after being in two foster homes. Her adopted mother was a nurse. Her natural mother was getting a divorce and the man she was remarrying did not want another man's child. She has two older brothers, also adopted (seven and eight years older, six months apart in age); one is an artist who has been on the missing person's list for years. Maggie bonded with her father, who died when she was 10. "Some part of me died when he died. My mother didn't tell me he died until after the funeral. I knew he was in the hospital and she wouldn't take me to see him."

The mother remarried when Maggie was 13. Maggie weighed 120 at the time of her father's death. Within two years, she weighed 225. Mother's new husband had a son who had sex in the afternoon with different people in front of her and masturbated all the time while she was around. "Mother never questioned why I hated him. My mother is like a black apple. I feel pain and darkness—no hope. Why bother? I'm tired. Nothing works. I feel pressure to not fail at therapy because I'll hurt and disappoint you. Same pressure in school—overwhelms and paralyzes me. I have wasted every gift I was given—that's why I deserve bad things. I don't know how this could have happened unless there's something wrong with me. If you can feel a piece of music that is me—then you can know me better. She gave me a tape of her favorite classical music, a combination of Beethoven, Vivaldi, Handel, and movie themes. I attract bad experiences because of being in a negative state—what you put out does come back to you."

I, the therapist, work hard at connection. There is a spark every now and then. I see a flash in Maggie's eyes that acknowledges that I am there. I feel morbid when I'm with her—I crave rest and sun. The connection process is so delicate and covered with black rot. I feel I'm with someone who is not pending death but already is dead and covered with an afterdeath. She is her own dead fetus. I have to provide meaningful existence for both of us when she is with me. Not only that, I have to obliterate the darkness first. When Maggie leaves, I open my office door to the outside. I take deep breaths.

November Notes: Catharsis of a Therapist

I'm trying to provide meaningful relatedness, processed through me to her lo gradually soften her dead inner environment. Maggie splits off her weak ego capacity to differentiate and integrate the alive and nonalive components of her life. She craves to establish some kind of sustained connection, symbiotic tie with me even though it seems somehow life threatening to her. She unconsciously knows her limited experience of symbiosis to be so destructive, she loses either way. She wants me to be more powerful so I can be a successful mother to her and pull her from withdrawal and autism.

I am becoming more and more in touch with the heaviness I feel at attempting to be nurturing. My feelings shift from tenderness to disgust. She activates my scorn and belittlement to such a degree that I wonder about myself. She comes into my office so full of superiority that I know within minutes she'll reduce me to feeling like a fraud. She fills the room with a hostile oozing energy that is full of vile hatred. In return, I find myself thinking: I hate you! I hate you! I hate working with you! You infect my practice. Go away—disappear—don't kill yourself; just get out of my space.

It's time to broach the all-important subject of how bad I feel when I'm with Maggie. She needs to be enlightened about how she affects me. The countertransference is so pervasive, I can hardly breathe. I know how hated she was. She needs to know I know, to feel that I have some sense of it. She needs to hear that I mourn her lost humanity and that I cringe at her deadening processes. I dread it won't go smoothly; nothing is smooth with her. There's potential for eruption always there; like a diabetic pus that won't heal. Gloom and doom. When she canceled an appointment I couldn't even feel good about that. There's no relief for me. There's always shit somewhere.

She can't always remember me in between sessions—I can't forget her! I have made her a tape of my voice and had her take a Polaroid photo of me to carry around. She has a pillow of mine. I don't know what else to do—give blood? Listen to my sarcasm.*

December Notes

Maggie has seemed docile and more connected to me for longer periods. I knew the time was as right as it would ever be. I basically said in words I hoped she would understand: "I have some very important things to share with you today. These are feelings, thoughts, observations about myself when I'm with you that may help us understand your difficulties even more. When you're very small and bad things happen, there are no words to describe or share with anyone because it is a preverbal period of our lives. The traumas and scary times become locked in our psyches and bodies and all we can do is cope defensively. We've worked on some of your defenses already; such as projection and denial. We have more to go, but today it is important to explore the feelings I have when I'm with you and even after you've left. Since there is no way for you to tell me just how terrible you feel, there is a therapeutic dance that goes on between us for you to show me somehow, someway, what goes on deep inside of you and you have shown me over and over.

"As we get to know one another I essentially become, in psychic experience, you the infant and you become your parents. Thus I come to know by living out your inner life. I know this sounds strange; but I also know you are extremely bright and will grasp this material. What I am developing is a fix on your very early development. You unconsciously become your parents; in particular your mother and foster mothers, and you act toward me as they did toward you. In this manner I become you as the infant. This is one of my jobs—to feel these emotions and share them with you and also to attempt to know what is not originating from my own personality dynamics. What is important is for us to know and understand your story. The powerful unconscious minds of both of us are at work here. When we are together, something different happens. We find out who we are more and more.

"Often and from the beginning, I experience intense feelings that are not common to me. I feel scared and confused around you. I feel I am not enough for you—that there is some awesome rage and chaos that I can't get out of easily. I feel depleted, drained of my life. I feel evil. As you listen to me, I'd like you to explore how this all might be representing your experience that is being made real to me. When I try to connect with you, I feel destroyed in my efforts. We know this is not your intention; not you, consciously. You are showing me something important. I even had a dream about this.

"There was a darling little blonde girl living around my house. She was so provocative and charming. She looked disheveled, though. I kept wanting to tidy her up. She was covered with something that had been there a long time, crusty and green. I was afraid to do that and knew it would take a long time. Somehow in this house my own mother was there. I loved the staircase because it was curving and graceful with a wooden bannister. My mother had it cut down to a horrid-looking stumpy stairs that didn't connect both floors. It looked awful and was crudely unfinished. I was very upset. The workmen were there defending it. I think this dream was about us and how our connection gets broken (the staircase) and how useless and helpless I am to make a significant difference. I offer so little comfort that you seem to be able to consistently use."

Maggie seemed somewhat dazed by this session and said she'd have to digest and listen to her music. I was so worried that her response wouldn't be constructive. The session had been very powerful. She said she felt okay leaving and that if she were overloaded, she would let me know. I checked on her later by phone.

The next session Maggie brought in two watercolor paintings that she said were provoked by our last meeting. One was a pregnant woman painted black with a fetus of blue with a red center. The other was a design with a dark center. She said, "This is what it's like to be in the black hole. It starts at the center and bleeds out, the black hole contains it, controls it, and won't let it live. Strong at the center, filters out and muddies anything that's good. I'm surrounded by this black hole. The world is buzzing around outside. I know you know something. I know you don't know what it's like to be there, but something's different about us. I feel calmer."

January Notes

"The environment seems colder. Right now I feel like if I came to see you every day it still wouldn't be enough to fill me up. That's part of the reason it's scary for me. When will it ever be enough? I feel like a bottomless pit. Therapy is like a Band-Aid when I really need surgery. I am wearing tense armor, ready to be attacked. I feel constantly under attack. I feel so bad in the morning. I have so many parts. They leave me when I need them. There's a part that could be really strong like at work. There's a part that could help me do it, but leaves me and doesn't come down and help me down to basics. One part is such a bitch, outer-directed and twisted. She sits on my shoulder waiting to jump my guard. I've stopped seeing the beauty. Beauty supported me before. My head is in the clouds. My sand dollar has started to decay. My mother will never love me. There's nothing I can do. Look at me, I'm so fat. I have the body of an old lady. My left leg shakes. The ghosts of the past are here. I hear a strong persecuting voice. When I get hungry, the voice says 'Don't eat.' When I do, I feel like throwing up. I've done something bad. This depression. I am naturally attracted to the turbulent dark side. It's very seductive. It's where I feel alive being drawn toward it; it becomes like the black hole drawing me even tighter and farther than before. It's getting out of control. Part of the wall between me and others is that I stop at that hole."

Maggie brought me her "bad stuff" in a brown paper bag. Bad stuff refers to her favorite movies: *The Killing Fields, Death of a Salesman, Crimes of the Heart, Holocaust, Escape from Salvador,* and *Desert Bloom.* She told me she left the important one at home.

February Notes

This month is a therapist's nightmare; my basic nightmare. Maggie's hearing battling voices. One says, "You're fat and ugly; a failure. You'll never be good; you're not good. You can never be good. I hate you!" The other voice says, "You must be perfect. You can't fail or she won't love you." Shutting up the voices is taking all of her energy. She called me and told me she wants to kill herself and believes she can. I convinced her to go immediately to her favorite doctor, a gynecologist who has seen her a number of times. He and I talk and he is very helpful in convincing her to seek a psychiatric evaluation immediately. (Notice how she relates to a man at this time.) She refused hospitalization and the psychiatrist says he cannot involuntarily commit her at this moment. He prescribed Prozac, 20 mg daily. The gynecologist gave her Xanax samples to calm her. She comes to therapy with her favorite video (the important one she had left at home before): *'Night, Mother.* She leaves it in my office to protect her from immediate suicide ideation and potential action. She reassures me that if I keep this video, she'll be safe.

'NIGHT, MOTHER

'Night, Mother is a play by Marsha Norman that won the Pulitzer Prize for drama in 1983. The subjects are suicide, love, and the meaning of life spoken in existential fashion. This disturbing play probes deeply into a mother-daughter symbiosis that ends in a suicide dance of the deepest despair and loneliness.

Of course, like the moth being attracted to the flame, Maggie happened upon this play in movie form, which, along with the original script, became her transitional object of sorts. She has read and watched it hundreds of times. The interaction between daughter Jessie and her Mama has struck a deep place within Maggie. She tells me it speaks to her like nothing else. She inadvertently discovered a replication of her internal script in the *'Night, Mother* dance of the two characters. She is addicted to the *'Night, Mother* interactions. She, like Jessie, wishes to die and knows that her life as she lives it has to end. Maggie even looks like Jessie, which probably increases her identification. She is sharing her guts with me in the form of this narrative. She is morbidly invested in every word. She wants me to join in.

Quotations from *'Night, Mother that* illustrate the bittersweet symbiotic interactions between Jessie and Mama:

Jessie: I'm going to kill myself, Mama.

Mama: Very funny. Very funny.

Jessie: I am.

Mama: You are not! Don't even say such a thing, Jessie.

Jessie: How would you know if I didn't say it? You want it to be a surprise. You're lying there in your bed or maybe you're just brushing your teeth and you hear this ... noise down the hall?

Mama: Kill yourself?

Jessie: Shoot myself. In a couple of hours.

Mama: It must be time for your medication.

Jessie: Took it already.

Mama: What's the matter with you?

Jessie: Not a thing. Feel fine.

Mama: You feel fine. You're just going to kill yourself.

Jessie: Waited until I feel good enough, in fact.

Mama: Don't make jokes, Jessie. I'm too old for jokes.

Jessie: It's not a joke, Mama.

Mama: You're not going to kill yourself, Jessie. You're not even upset! (Jessie smiles or laughs quietly, and Mama tries a different approach.) People don't really kill themselves Jessie. No ma'am, doesn't make sense, unless you're retarded or deranged, and you're as normal as they come, Jessie, for the most part. We're all afraid to die.

Jessie: I'm not Mama. I'm cold all the time, anyway.

Mama: That's ridiculous.

Jessie: It's exactly what I want. It's dark and quiet.

Mama: So is the backyard, Jessie. Close your eyes. Stuff cotton in your ears. Take a nap! It's quiet in your room. I'll leave the T.V. off all night.

Jessie: So quiet I don't know it's quiet. So nobody can get me.

Mama: You don't know what dead is like. It might not be quiet at all. What if it's like an alarm clock and you can't wake up so you can't shut it off. Ever.

Jessie: Dead is everybody and everything I ever knew, gone. Dead is dead quiet.

Mama: It's a sin. You'll go to hell.

Jessie: Uh-huh.

Mama: You will!

Jessie: Jesus was a suicide, if you ask me.

Mama: You'll go to hell just for saying that, Jessie.

Jessie: Mama ... I'm just not having a very good time and I don't have any reason to think it'll get anything but worse. I'm tired. I'm hurt. I'm sad. I feel used.

Mama: Tired of what?

Jessie: It all.

Mama: What does that mean?

Jessie: I can't say it any better.

Mama: There's nothing real sad going on right now. If it was after your divorce or something, that would make sense.

Jessie: I can't do anything about my life, to change it, make it better, make it work. But I can stop it. Shut it down, turn it off like the radio when there's nothing on I want to listen to. It's all I really have that belongs to me and I'm going to say what happens to it. And it's going to stop. And I'm going to stop it. So, let's just have a good time.

Mama: Have a good time!

Jessie: We can't go on fussing all night. I mean, I could ask you things I always wanted to know and you could make me some hot chocolate. The old way.

Mama: Why did Cecil leave you?

Jessie: Cecil left me because he made me choose between him and smoking.

Mama: Jessie, I know he wasn't that dumb.

Jessie: Smoking is the only thing I know that's always just what you think it's going to be. Just like it was the last time, right there when you want it and real quiet.

Jessie: (Standing up) It's time for me to go, Mama.

Mama: (Starting for her) No, Jessie, you've got all night!

Jessie: (As Mama grabs her) No, Mama. '

Mama: It's not even ten o'clock.

Jessie: (Very calm) Let me go, Mama.

Mama: I can't. You can't go. You can't do this. You didn't say it would be so soon, Jessie. I'm scared. I love you.

Jessie: (Takes her hand away) Let go of me, Mama. I've said everything I had to say.

Mama: (Standing still a minute) You said you wanted to do my nails.

Jessie: (Taking a small step backward) I can't. It's too late.

Mama: It's not too late!

Jessie: Don't try and stop me, Mama, you can't do it.

Mama: (Grabbing her again, this time hard) I can too! I'll stand in front of this hall and you can't get past me. (They struggle.) You'll have to knock me down to get away from me, Jessie. I'm not about to let you ...

Jessie: (Almost a whisper) 'Night, Mother. (She vanishes into her bedroom and *we* hear the door lock just as Mama gets to it.)

Mama: (Screams) Jessie! (Pounding on the door.) Jessie, you let me in there. Don't you do this, Jessie. I'm not going to stop screaming until you open this door, Jessie. Jessie! Jessie! Stop this! I didn't know! I was here with you all the time. How could I know you were so alone? (And Mama stops for a moment, breathless and frantic, putting her ear to the door, and when she doesn't hear anything, she stands up straight again and screams once more.) Jessie! Please! (And we hear the shot, and it sounds like an answer, it sounds like NO. Mama collapses against the door, tears streaming down her face, but not screaming anymore. In shock now.) Jessie, Jessie, child ... Forgive me. (Pause) I thought you were mine.

Maggie wants me to play *'Night, Mother* with her. She has wanted this from the start. Of course, she couldn't tell me this. Watching the movie and reading the script has enlightened me. I feel like I've been struck in the head by lightning bolts. She carries the video around in a paper bag. She leaves it in my office for safekeeping with a great deal of pomp and circumstance. She tells me that as long as I have *'Night, Mother* in my possession, she won't do anything. She promises to leave it with me for so many weeks, then asks for it in the next session. Keep this dangerous movie away from me, she begs and then sneers at me and insists on having it back that instant! It's as if she gives me something precious then takes it away with sadistic pleasure. In spite of the rich material we discuss at length, the obsession exhausts us both.

I've had it with this *'Night, Mother* spook show. I hate feeling responsible for keeping Maggie alive, as if I could. I know the agony of Mama. It's my turn to let her know how much I detest being in this position. The dialogue from that session went like this: "I really want to relate to you in a warm and caring way. As long as I've known you, and before, you've been on a suicide course. I can't be warm and caring when you turn me into a hospital or police person whose job is to keep you from killing yourself. I don't want that job! I didn't train or sign up for that job. Your most important way to relate to life is in *'Night, Mother* games. I cannot play it with you. I will not be your " 'Night, Mother." It's not right for me. You've got to stop this! When you endanger your life, you can't have me. The hospital is *'Night, Mother.* The hospital's job is to keep you from killing yourself. Jessie had the last word with Mama, the blast of a gun. I know you're looking for a way to have the last word with me. You can have the last word. I just want to be free to do the work that needs to be done. I really want to relate to you. We can connect in a real way; as two warm loving humans." I gave her a candle from my office to light whenever she wanted to know I was there. She put it in her brown paper bag.

Maggie said somehow our last session when "I blew up at her" helped her to get some things into a new perspective, that she could feel me better.

She watched *'Night, Mother* again. She told me she could always really identify with Jessie's logic about killing herself. But this time she saw a girl who had lived a lifetime of pain that she never expressed to anyone and how no one picked up on her pain, so they thought everything was fine. She also saw someone who was already dead basically; that killing herself just the completion of the physical act of something that had long been dead. She told me she now knows I know all this. She saw someone who was always taking care of all the chores and taking care of her mother. Even as she was going to kill herself, she continued to be responsible. It was as if she wanted to leave this world with as little mess as possible and without causing anybody any trouble. Like she just wants to slip away without a ripple, like the divers do when they do a perfect dive, without a ripple; without being noticed. "If you turned your back," she said, "you would never see it." It's like she had lived her life; she hadn't been noticed—made no impact at all. She saw someone who had been so hurt all her life, yet had not given voice to that pain until that one evening when all or part of it came out.

Maggie told me that now she sees why she identifies with that movie so much. Before she was not in touch with her feelings, yet she knew something important about her. Now, she says, just thinking about it gives her this anxious feeling in the pit of her stomach like something really bad is going to happen only she doesn't know quite what it is. Her hands become sweaty and she feels really nervous. Now, she's going to read the script again to see if she can experience it from a different perspective. She says that she can intellectually kind of understand where the mother is coming from, but mostly feels totally cut off from her and her feelings of pain, excuses, and reasons.

She told me she had the thought hit that what if she decided she'd had enough of this life and decided to kill herself because it seems like too much hell. And she killed herself only to find out that she was already in hell and that killing herself just got her a ticket to the same place. It would be horrible to realize that she was in hell all along and she thought it was just a really bad life!

May Notes

Maggie brought in dreams. First one: "I'm holding a baby. Did I have it or was it given to me? I didn't breast-feed. That's how I knew I didn't have the baby. The baby should eat now. I am confused, so I asked someone which formula is the best to feed."

Second dream: "I'm in an old house with an old man. The house was going to tumble down. Leave this. Leave this. I'm trying to stuff in a suitcase Christmas ornaments—clear balls with fish in them—going up to the top to get air."

Third dream, which is recurring: "I'm saving fish that are almost dead. I'm having one minute left to save them."

She reports feeling more balanced. She even smiles at me now I told Maggie I wish there was some consistent way to reach out to her and some way for her to connect with my reaching out. She said she almost trusts me; that she trusts my insides and some small consistent actions that aren't always there. She can't find the words to explain. Words don't do any good. She's afraid I'll start beating her. She says she can see the craziness of *'Night, Mother* now and that she used to feel a victim of it.

July Notes

Maggie wants me to help her construct affirmations. I gave her: "I am a child of the universe. I have a right to be here on earth. I am a loving person." She told me she leaves here feeling more empty than when she comes. "I get stuck in between me and her; so divided and vivid. 'Her' is culturally fancy; is judgmental, can't condescend; is perfect. 'Me' is nothing." She wants her *'Night, Mother* video back. Says she can manage the feelings now. Dream: "I am on a bridge of feeling and you're my fairy godmother and this place isn't real and you can't do it for me, but you can help me understand and realize things. Then a bobcat appeared and wanted to kill an animal. I felt strong in the dream."

August Notes

"In the last couple of months I feel full sometimes. If I had known what it was going to take to get me here, I would have killed myself. It wasn't worth it; even as good as I feel now, compared to before. Once a week, I have energy—rumor has it that I may make it." Dream: "A friend and a baby are on a porch. My grandmother looks dead, but twitches. My brother and mother were there and said, she's dead. Twitching is normal. Grandmother's not dead—she gets up and walks around."

September Notes

Suicidal thoughts are different now, not as threatening. Maggie has "logical tapes" that stop the thoughts. She has developed enough of a false self or an observing ego now to monitor the warring voices of inner child and demonic parents. She began two college classes and ended up dropping both. Dream: "I asked you what do you think of your daughter? You said, 'I couldn't do without her. She's so good.'"

She wants a clean break from therapy. She can't afford the money or the pain of connecting. So we've been in termination process for two months now. By now Maggie has a large bill with me. Because she has so desperately needed therapy and because I have feared for her life, I have been very kind about not receiving payments. She owes me $5,000. I have helped her file for insurance several times and nothing remunerative happens; the insurance company stalls and denies payment for various reasons. I feel almost too tired to go after this account. She has no money and I don't press her now either. I am usually competent at solving insurance dilemmas and staying on top of accounts. Once again, I am the infant via the counter-transference that cannot wage a battle against the all-powerful and withholding parent insurance company.

Now comes the final chapter. Maggie filed for bankruptcy. I received a notice in the mail two months after our last session. Balance zero. Her whereabouts unknown. It's as if the therapy was her birthright—that she shouldn't have to pay to exist in my office or anyone else's office. She did have the last word. I could hear her say to me "'Night, you fool." What she owed me is really what was owed to her in nature a thousand times over: a real mother with goodness and love. Emotional bankruptcy was filed on her a long time ago. She played it out to the bitter end.

Perhaps writing this vignette helps me let go. I thank Maggie for the invaluable lessons and poignant experiences of my own inner world. Because the therapy was not able to reach some kind of natural completion, not to mention the unpaid bill, I realize it was inevitable for me to feel frustrated as well as useful and nurturing. I am far wiser in my understanding of what takes place on a primitive level. For this I am grateful. From the position Maggie left me in I can now say, knowing what it means to her, "Good night, Mother." But at least it is I who am symbolically left for dead and she, as survivor, is on her own to find her way in the world. Wherever Maggie is, I wish her well.

Chapter Ten
Liability and Risk Management

In 1990, due to the escalation of licensing board complaints and malpractice suits against therapists I took on the task of teaching Law and Ethics Continuing Education classes for licensed psychotherapists and have taught a dozen or more such classes each year in a number of states and Canada ever since. In 2000 I first published a comprehensive text for therapists, *Facing the Challenge of Liability: Practicing Defensively*. In 2007 I published a revised and expanded edition of that book—a book that because of its topic has not proven very popular! In the forward Bryant Welch, the attorney-psychoanalyst who first established the APA Practice Directorate wrote: "Malpractice lawsuits and licensing board complaints are a serious threat to the welfare of psychotherapists. It is a fantasy to think that only the culpable are brought before licensing boards or become the targets of malpractice litigation. Being a good person and a competent therapist does not guarantee that one will not be forced to defend the profession, often with the very right to continue practicing at stake. Anyone who works with borderline patients, families, children, or very sick patients is at risk. It is that simple, and it is only at one's peril that one denies this fact. In reading Dr. Hedges' latest work, we can take a meaningful step out of the confusion that surrounds many psychotherapists today about the source and nature of their vulnerability before licensure boards and malpractice tribunals."

In *Facing the Challenge of Liability* I dealt with the basics of false accusations against therapists and suicide prevention. But suicide had not yet been declared a "national epidemic". With the current book I have hopefully expanded our awareness of the many complex dimensions of suicidality and in this closing chapter I return to the task of facing our liability and, most of all, *practicing defensively*. In the following paragraphs I reprint my earlier basic advice before we go on to consider how our liability regarding suicide has rapidly expanded since:

> Considering and predicting suicide risk is one of the most widely researched areas in psychology. While many interesting and objective scales and tests have been devised, unfortunately, massive research continues to demonstrate to date that *there are no valid and reliable ways* of predicting non-lethal or lethal suicidal behavior.[215] *But there are many important known risk factors that every clinician must be familiar with and consider in her/his clinical assessment of how to handle the dangers.*

Suicide Contracts and Precautions against Self-Abusive Activities

> Suicide and self-abuse contracts alone are an insufficient standard of care. Common sense requires that you regularly do risk assessments and take emergency measures if the risk is high. If the risk is moderate, you must mobilize social and family support. If the risk is low, you can continue with careful follow-up. While most attorneys want us to document all suicidal and self-abusive gestures and risks carefully in our notes, some experts point out that a documented risk assessment immediately before a seriously damaging or successful suicide attempt could put us in potential jeopardy. But

---

[215] While there are many fine books on suicide risk, the book which presents the most comprehensive review of the literature and available research to date is *Assessment, Treatment, and Prevention of Suicidal Behavior* edited by Robert I. Yufit and David Lester with a forward by foremost suicidologist Norman Farberow (Wiley, 2005).

we want to err on the side of safety. It is always best to document carefully and to seek immediate peer and specialty consultation to cover yourself. You can more easily be defended for a well-reasoned, good-faith breach of confidentiality in a clearly dangerous circumstance than for suicide, homicide, or for serious self or other injury.

All therapists need ongoing continuing education in the area of suicide risk management since research findings continue to expand this critical area of practice. Make it a point whenever you see a book, and article, a workshop or an on-line course on suicide prevention to take it and to keep documentation of your ongoing training experiences since there is no clearly fixed knowledge base or tried and true guidelines in this area.

Another way of documenting your ongoing training in this or any speciality area is to download articles and file them in your Continuing Education folder and/or in a particular client's record—that way your efforts will be documented and dated.

Suicide Lability Risk Management: A Summary
Psychologist/attorney Bryant L. Welch lists eight areas of ongoing concern.[216]

1. Do an initial comprehensive suicide risk assessment of the patient and make assessment an ongoing part of treatment. Be mindful of the suicide risk factors, tapping the latest available literature on the subject.
2. Don't allow yourself to deny a suicide risk.
3. Spend adequate time with the patient—whether you get paid for all
of it or not.
4. If necessary, make it clear to the managed care company that a lack of treatment could be seen as negligence and result in a lawsuit against them—put this in a certified letter to the

---

[216] Welch (2000).

managed care representative if necessary.

5. Practice full disclosure with the family of the suicidal patient.
6. Educate the patient's family about the signs of potential suicide.
7. Employ good follow-up practices with patients.
8. Always follow good documentation procedures.

Pope and Vasquez list what continue to be critical areas to evaluate in determining the risk of a suicide.[217]

1. A direct verbal warning is the single most useful predictor.
2. The presence of a plan increases the risk.
3. Eighty percent of completed suicide attempts have been preceded by previous attempts.
4. People give away their plans by indirect references.
5. Depression is a significant predictor; 15 percent of clinically depressed people kill themselves.
6. Hopelessness is highly associated with suicide intent.
7. One-fourth to one-third of successful suicides are associated with drug or alcohol intoxication.
8. Suicide rates are higher in diagnosable clinical syndromes such as

depression, alcoholism, primary mood disorders, and schizophrenia—and with relatives of clients who have committed suicide.

9. The suicide rate for men is three times greater than for women, and five times higher for young men.
10. Suicide risk increases with age and the life cycle, peaking between the mid-50s to the mid-60s.
11. In the United States Caucasians have the highest rate.
12. Suicide rates are higher among Protestants than among Jews and Catholics.
13. The risk is highest for those living alone, less if living with a spouse, and less if there are children.
14. Bereavement over lost loved ones in recent years increases

---

[217] Pope & Vasquez (1991).

the risk.

15. Unemployment increases the suicide risk.

16. Illness and somatic complaints, just like sleep and eating disturbances, increase the risk.

17. Those with high impulsivity are at increased risk for taking their own lives.

18. Rigid thinking increases the risk, for example, a person who says such things as, "If I don't find work in the next week the only real alternative is to kill myself."

19. Any stressful event is likely to destabilize a person, putting her or him at higher risk for suicide.

20. The risk is greater after weekend hospital leaves and after being discharged from a hospital.

Clients who engage in chronic and intractable suicidal gestures, self-injuring activities, or other potentially self-abusive or harmful behaviors may need to be terminated and referred out of individual psychotherapy on the basis of unmanageability. The resources we have at our disposal often do not meet the client's needs. This must be explained to the client early in therapy, and limits must be set and put into writing with consequences that are effectively followed through on. I have seen many therapists struggle compassionately for long periods of time with clients, making clear in a no-fault, non-punitive fashion that they are not equipped to deal with such intense and dangerous expressions, so that these forms of communication have to be renounced in order for therapy to continue.

I find that it is usually the therapist's resistance to limit-setting and systematic follow-through that slows down the process. But the bottom line is that no therapist is in a personal or professional position to receive endlessly or to respond effectively to chronic life-threatening or safety-endangering communications.

If it is not possible to contain the therapy work in manageable limits, the client must be referred to a more appropriate intensive therapeutic resource or to a setting where different liability parameters exist. Almost all clients confronted in this seemingly harsh way about how important their therapy work is, how crucial safe and manageable nonthreatening communications are for the sanity and well-being of the therapist, and how the client must find alternative forms of experiencing and communicating her or his concerns, in fact, do find different, creative, and contained ways of continuing their therapy work with the therapist safely. But the therapist has to believe that alternate forms of communication are essential for mutual safety and that they are achievable within the creative potential of the client for the limit setting to work effectively. If the client truly cannot comply in this way your liability is simply too great to continue with her or him.

Earlier in the present book I further gave some representative statistics of risk factors and risk populations that are important to consider.

The book, hands down, which gives the most concise and carefully considered approach to the current situation of risk and liability in suicidality and that contains numerous forms for assessment and treatment of suicidality is David Rudd's *The Assessment and Management of Suicidality*.[218] A close runner up is *Assessing and Managing Risk in Psychological Practice* published by the APA Insurance Trust.[219] Both of these books are readily available through Amazon and *I highly recommend that every clinician have both of them within hand's reach* because we never know when a suicidal crisis will plop down in the chair opposite us! And there are so many factors to consider that none of us can keep them in our minds, much less on the tip of our tongues—

---

[218] Rudd (2006).
[219] Bennett et al. (2006).

especially during a busy treatment day!

Since, as previously discussed, we have no fully reliable methods of predicting or preventing suicidal acts, the standards of practice with regard to suicidality tend to be fluid on a case-to-case basis and largely established *after the fact* in court or licensing board hearings by expert witnesses who will raise a series of trenchant questions designed to make any of us look quite unprofessional. *Our only option at this point in time is to take a deep breath and get serious about protecting ourselves from serious accusations of unprofessional conduct.* Writes Rudd, who has served repeatedly as an expert witness and been up against a number of other very sharp expert witnesses:

> When a life is tragically lost to suicide, it is imperative that the clinician be able to provide documentation offering a clear, specific, and succinct rationale for clinical decisions. Trust me, a host of questions will be directed at the practitioner:
>
> 1. Why was a patient who was thinking about suicide or had made a suicide attempt not hospitalized?
> 2. Why was a given course of treatment followed when there were indications that the patient was not responding well or getting better?
> 3. Did you consider alternative treatment options?
> 4. Was medication considered?
> 5. What did you do to safeguard the patient's environment?
> 6. What steps were taken in response to the identified risk level?
> 7. Did you make an effort to talk with and enlist the help of family and friends?
> 8. Did the patient have a crisis response plan in place to deal with unexpected crises?
>
> It is important to understand that the standard of care is a fluid construct, one defined independently for each

claim and case of malpractice or negligence. Ultimately it is defined by the expert witness testifying in court. Nevertheless, there still are common elements, including (a) foreseeability, (b) treatment planning, and (c) follow-up or follow-through (Jobes & Berman, 1993). This book was written with these common elements in mind, particularly the issue of hindsight bias and perceived foreseeability. In many forensic cases, the issue of foreseeability is confused with the issue of predictability. More specifically, as clinicians, many of us believe that we can somehow predict individual suicides. There is ample scientific evidence that low base-rate problems like suicide cannot be meaningfully predicted on an individual basis (cf. Pokorny, 1992). Regardless, the expectation persists, and all practitioners should keep this in mind.

Although we cannot reliably predict individual suicides, we can determine periods of heightened risk, what Litman (1989) referred to as the *suicide zone*. When we have recognized escalating risk, we need to respond accordingly and then continue to monitor the situation and respond in accordance with subsequent clinical markers until risk resolves. If we refer someone out for further evaluation or treatment, we need to follow up and see if the referral was kept. If not, we need to explore why not. If the acute suicidal state continues, then we again need to respond as clinically indicated. This is a clinical application of the three elements of the standard of practice in suicidality: foreseeability, treatment planning, and follow-up. These three elements apply regardless of whether or not we see a patient one time or twenty. It is essential that we complete thorough and accurate risk assessments (foreseeability), respond appropriately (treatment planning), and make sure our plan was implemented (follow- up) even if we are not the one providing the continuing care.[220]

Rudd begins his small cogent volume with various definitions of suicidality and what kinds of activities warrant what kinds of responses from clinicians.

He cites O'Carroll et al. (1996) in noting that suicidal behavior can be distinguished by three characteristic features: intent to die, evidence of self-infliction, and outcome (injury, no injury, or death). Those suicidologists have offered clear definitions of suicide; suicide attempts with injuries; suicide attempts without injuries; instrumental suicide-related behavior; potentially self-injurious behavior for which there is evidence (either implicit or explicit) that the person did not intend to kill himself/herself with injuries; without injuries; or with fatal outcome (i.e., accidental death); suicidal threat; and suicidal ideation.[221] Rudd continues:

> When thinking about differentiating among suicide attempts, instrumental behavior, and suicide threats, the critical variable to consider is intent. You can think about intent in two overlapping, but not identical, ways. First, there is subjective or *expressed* intent. This is what the patient says to you. Did the patient say he or she wants (wanted) to kill himself or herself? Be sure to document exactly what the patient said; directly quoting the patient is preferred and recommended (e.g., *I'm going to shoot myself or I wish I had died from taking the pills*). Second, there is objective or observed intent. This is essentially what the patient does, that is, concrete behavior you observe. Again, describe the behavior in simple and direct terms. Did the patient prepare for suicide (e.g., write letters to children, parents, a spouse; get financial

---

220 Rudd, op. cit., p. 4.

221 O'Carroll et al. (1996), pp. 240-241.

documents in order, revise a will)? Did he or she take actions to prevent discovery and/or rescue? Was the attempt in an isolated, secluded, or protected area? Was the attempt timed in such a way as to prevent discovery (e.g.. when the patient knew no one would be home for hours or days)? Was rescue and intervention only by random chance? Markers of objective intent include behaviors that demonstrate

- a desire to die,
- preparation tor death (e.g., letters to loved ones, organizing financial records, obtaining or modifying insurance policies, writing or revising a will), and
- efforts to prevent discovery or rescue.... [p. 9]

Think back about the essential elements of the standard of care; the issue of foreseeability is a challenging one, particularly in cases of chronic suicide risk or what Maris (1992) referred to as "suicidal careers." Consistent with Litman's (1989) notion of the suicide zone, suicide risk varies over time; periods of heightened risk come and go, even for those individuals who are considered at chronic risk. It is important to have a conceptual model for understanding suicide risk over time; this is essential prior to talking about the content of the assessment. Such a conceptual model helps guide the process of risk assessment with a patient over time, making clinical decisions straightforward even for those with long suicidal histories.... [p. 13]

In short, the clinician should be aware that when a patient has a history' of multiple suicide attempts, the clinician will need to talk about chronic risk in his or her writeup. Even though acute symptoms and intent have subsided, the patient's heightened susceptibility to future suicidal crises has not. This needs to be acknowledged in the chart. If it is not specifically stated that the patient poses a chronic risk for suicide, then the implicit (and wrong) assumption is that that the patient is not at risk once the acute crisis (i.e., acute symptoms) has resolved. Acknowledging chronic risk for a patient indicates that the threshold for intensive care and intervention for this patient is different than for others. It recognizes that these individuals have enduring vulnerabilities that cannot be effectively treated by inpatient or other acute care alternatives. Such enduring vulnerabilities are only effectively treated over longer periods of time.

In short, a thorough assessment of suicide risk demands that the clinician address both acute and chronic features of the patient's [p. 16] suicidality.

Rudd distinguishes clearly between acute and chronic suicide risks and the clinician's obligations in both cases. He elaborates: precipitant, nature of ideation or attempt, outcome, and reaction. Throughout his book he gives lists of crucial questions for clinicians to ask in order to determine various kinds and levels of suicidality and risk.

The final area relevant to the specifics of suicidal thinking is protective factors. It is important for the clinician to have a clear understanding of what protective factors are in place for the patient—that are available and accessible during periods of acute crisis. Most important among protective factors are social support and an active treatment relationship (cf. Rudd et al., 2004). Protective factors can be captured with the following questions:

- Even though you've had a very difficult time, something kept you going. What are your reasons for living?
- Are you hopeful about the future?
- What would need to happen to help you be more hopeful about the future?
- What keeps you going in difficult times like this?
- Whom do you rely on during difficult times?
- Has treatment been effective for you in the past? [p. 33]

Since I believe that Rudd's guidebook is important enough that everyone should have near at hand, I am going to simply list the kinds of very helpful tables and appendices he offers so you can see the great utility of this book.

TABLE 1: Additional Areas of Risk Assessment[222]

I: Predisposition to Suicidal Behavior [numerous factors listed]

II: Identifiable Precipitant or Stressors [listed]

III: Symptomatic Presentation (have patient rate severity on 1-10 scale) [listed]

IV: Presence of Hopelessness (have patient rate severity on 1-10 scale) [scales listed]

V: The Nature of Suicidal Thinking [kinds described]

VI: Previous Suicidal Behavior

VII: Impulsivity and Self-Control (have patient rate on 1-10 scale)

VIII: Protective Factors

TABLE 2: Acute Suicide Risk Continuum

Risk Level Description [Mild, minimal, moderate, severe, extreme—with steps to follow in each case]

The Commitment to Treatment Statement

[The general dimensions of a Commitment to Treatment Statement are outlined and Rudd gives an example of the one he uses.]

The Crisis Response Plan

[to be individualized with each client with example things to do on

---

[222] Ibid. Table elaborated helpfully beginning on p. 41.

his or her own when the person is thinking or acting suicidal]

The Importance of Documentation:

Open and Closed Risk Markers [Listing of kinds of markers that should be carefully documented]

Consultation: Knowing When to Ask for Help

[A series of important considerations of the kinds of situations that should raise questions needing consultation]

Points To Remember for the Practicing Clinician [Review list]

Appendix A: Standard Suicide Risk Assessment Form

Appendix B: Sample Commitment to Treatment Statement

Appendix C: Sample Crisis Response Plan

As you can see David Rudd's *The Assessment and Management of Suicidality* is a must have and must read for all practicing clinicians!

Chapter Eleven
Conclusions: Managing Suicidality in Clinical Settings

After exhaustive research and thought there are a series of conclusions:

1. Despite two hundred years of widespread attention and six decades of intensive scientific study, our overall ability to predict and prevent suicide is now seen as no better than chance.

2. Research studying various populations aimed at establishing "risk factors", biological factors, familial or social factors are helpful in identifying high risk situations but fail at targeting the individual psychodynamics of suicidal individuals.

3. "Suicide crisis" therapies embarked on in the short "window of vulnerability" following a suicide attempt are often successful in reducing suicidal ideation in the short-term but do not address the long-term underlying suicidal dynamics.

4. Expert suicidologists from around the world generally endorse the Aeschi imperative that a "therapeutic alliance" must be formed with suicidal people with the goal of engaging them in long-term therapy.

5. Suicidologists generally agree that—despite the appearance of loneliness and isolation—suicidality is always dyadic in nature.

6. The therapeutic approaches that claim clinical or empirical successes are strikingly similar in that they address the "suicidal career"—the life-long recursive relational patterns underlying suicidality.

7. While suicidality often represents a "cry for help", at the epicenter is unbearable "Psycheache" and a "cry of pain".

8. Suicidologists around the world have identified trauma in early child development—especially abuse and abandonment—as the psychodynamic sources of suicidality.

9. Suicidologists have been uniform in calling for a developmental theory to account for how the early seeds of suicidality are laid down.

10. The psychoanalysts, the Jungians, the DBT group let by Linehan, the TFP group led by Kernberg, the Relational Listening group led by Hedges, and the Austin-Riggs group have in common that they generally see *intentional completed suicides* as stemming from psychotic, mood-disordered, or autistic spectrum states that require intense psychodynamic and psychiatric treatment.

11. These same groups of treatment experts have in common that they see most *instrumental suicidal gestures and attempts* as stemming from characterological states such as borderline, addictive, and sociopathic personality disorders.

12. All approaches—clinical and empirical—that claim long-term therapeutic success are based on forming a strong "therapeutic alliance" with an extensive "working through"

that promotes significant personality transformation.

13. All therapeutic approaches to suicidality modify traditional "therapeutic neutrality," in that realistic instructions, contracts, and life interventions must be undertaken in times of suicidal crisis.

14. The *Relational Listening* approach developed over 40 years by a large group of psychodynamic therapists in Southern California targets the "Organizing" developmental relatedness mode as the psychodynamic source of most *intentional completed suicides*.

15. The *Relational Listening* approach targets the "Symbiotic" developmental relatedness mode as the psychodynamic source of most *instrumental suicidal gestures and attempts*.

16. All of the leading therapeutic approaches have in common an in-depth, detailed inquiry into the life-history and relational-history of the suicidal person.

17. The leading therapeutic approaches generally recognize that the reasons given and the narratives engaged in by the suicidal person are a conscious overlay to the deep unconscious relational sources of suicidality.

18. The *Relational Listening* approach currently offers the only clear and explicit theory of early child development to account for *intentional completed suicides* as well as *instrumental suicidal gestures and attempts*.

19. Any systematic therapeutic approach that allows for a long-term therapeutic alliance engaged in a detailed life inquiry focusing on relationships will likely have the power to

transform the personality so that suicidality is no longer an issue.

References

American Association of Suicidology. (2016). African American Suicide Fact Sheet based on 2014 data. www.wellspacehealth.org, retrieved 1-1-18.

American Psychological Association. (2000). *Report from the APA Working Group on Assisted Suicide and End-of-Life Decisions.* http://www.apa.org/pubs/info/reports/aseol.aspx, retrieved 1-1-18.

____ (2001). Retrieved from website 1/1/18. Suicide by profession: lots of confusion, inconclusive data.

____ (2005). Retrieved from website 1/1/18. Suicide prevention is a top White House priority.

____ (2008). Retrieved from website 1/1/18. Preventing teen suicide through *familias.*

____ (2010). Retrieved from website 1/1/18. Military suicides continue to climb.

____ (2014). Retrieved from website 1/1/18. Trauma Before Enlistment Linked to High Suicide Rates Among Military Personnel, Veterans, Research Finds.

____ (2016). Retrieved from website 1/1/18. CDC Releases Sexual Minority Youth Data.

____ (2017), Retrieved from website 1/1/18. Rurality's relationship to suicide risk. [An interview with Kendra Thorne].

____ (2018), Retrieved from website 1/1/18. Suicide among Asian-Americans: Myths about suicides among Asian-Americans.

____ (2018). Retrieved from website 1/1/18. Suicide and bullying.

Alvarez, A. (1971). *The Savage God: A study of Suicide.* New York: Scribner.

Balint, A. (1943). Identification. *Int. J. Psycho-Anal.,* 24:97-107.

Birtchnell, J. (1983). Psychotherapeutic Considerations in the Management of the Suicidal Patient. *American Journal of Psychotherapy,* 37:24-36.

Bennett, B. E., Bricklin, P. M., Harris, E., Knapp, S., VandeCreek, L., and

Youngren, J. N. (2006). *Assessing and Managing Risk in Psychological Practice: An Individualized Approach.* Rockville, MD: The Trust.

Blauner, S. (2002). *How I Stayed Alive When My Brain Was Trying to Kill Me: One Person's Guide to Suicide Prevention.* New York: Harper Collins.

Bollas, C. (1987). *The Shadow of the Object: Psychoanalysis of the Unthought Known.* London: Free Association Books.

Bromberg, P. (2011). *The Shadow Of The Tsunami And The Growth Of The Relational Mind*: New York: Routledge.

Bowlby, J. (1983) *Attachment and Loss, Vol. 1.* New York:Basic Books.

Burton, R. (1621). *The Anatomy of Mealancholy.* (Kindle version).

Cain, A. (1972). *Survivors of Suicide.* Springfield, IL: Charles C Thomas.

Crook, M. (2004). *Out of the Darkness: Teens Talk About Suicide.* (Kindle version).

Durkheim, E. (1879). *Suicide.* 1997, New York: Free Press.

Franklin, J., Ribiero, J., Fox, A. Kleinman, E, Jaroszewski, A., Nock, M. Bentley, K., Huang, X., Musacchio, and K. Chang, B. (2016). risk factors for suicidal thoughts and behaviors: A meta-analysis of 50 years of research. *Psychological Bulletin*, published online Nov. 14, 2016.

Freud, A. (1967). About losing and being lost. *Psychoanaly. Study Child*, 22:9-19.

S. Freud (1901). *The Psychopathology of Everyday Life. Standard Edition.* 6:178-185

____ (1910). Contributions to a discussion on suicide. *Standard Edition.* 11:232.

____ (1914). Recollecting, repeating and working through (further recommendations on the technique of psycho-analysis II). *Standard Edition.* 12:145-156.

____ (1917). Mourning and melancholia, *The Standard Edition.* 14:237-258.

____ (1920). The psychogenesis of a case of homosexuality in a woman. *Standard Edition.* 18: 147-172.

____ (1923). *The Ego and the Id. Standard Edition.* 19:49.

____ (1938). The splitting of the ego in the process of defense. *Standard Edition*. 23:271-278.

____ (1940). An Outline of Psychoanalysis. *Standard Edition*. 23:148-150.

Gaines, R. (1997). Detachment And Continuity: The Two Tasks of Mourning. *Contemporary Psychoanalysis*, 33:549-571, Kindle version.

Green, A. (1986). The dead mother. In *On Private Madness pp142-170*.

Halbwachs, M. (1930). *The Causes of Suicide*. London and Henley: Routledge & Kegan Paul (Trans. Harold Goldblat).

Hedges, L. (1983). *Listening Perspectives in Psychotherapy*. Northvale, NJ: Jason Aronson Publishers [Twentieth Anniversary Edition, 2003].

____ (1994). *In Search of the Lost Mother of Infancy*. Northvale, NJ: Jason Aronson Publishers.

____ (1996). *Strategic Emotional Involvement: Using Countertransference Experience in Psychotherapy*. Northvale, NJ: Jason Aronson Publishers.

____ (2012). *Overcoming Relationship Fears*. International Psychotherapy Institute e-Book, freepsychotherapybooks.org.

____ (2013). *Overcoming Relationship Fears Workbook*. International Psychotherapy Institution e-Book, freepsychotherapybooks.org.

____ (2015). *Facing Our Developmental Traumas*. International Psychotherapy Institute e-Book, freepsychotherapybooks.org.

____ (2018). *Relational Listening*. International Psychotherapy Institute e-Book, freepsychotherapybooks.org.

____ (1997). Hedges, L., Hilton, R., Hilton, V., and Caudill, B. *Therapists at Risk: Perils of the Intimacy of the Therapeutic Relationship*. Northvale, NJ: Jason Aronson Publishers.

Hendin, H. (1969). *Black Suicide*. New York: Basic Books.

Hillman, J. (1965/2011). *Suicide and the Soul*. Putnam, CT: Spring Publications.

Holmes, J. (2011). Attachment Theory and the Suicidal Patient. In Michel, K., and Jobes, D. A. *Building a Therapeutic Alliance with the Suicidal Patient*. Washington, D.C.: American Psychological Association.

Jamison, K. R. (1999). *Night Falls Fast: Understanding Suicide*. New York: Alfred A. Knopf.

Jensen, V., and Petty, T. (1996). The fantasy of being rescued in suicide. In Maltsberger, J., and Goldblatt, M. (1996). *Essential Papers on Suicide.* New York: New York University Press, pp 131-141.

Jobes, D. (2011). Suicidal patients, the therapeutic alliance, and the collaborative assessment and management of suicidality. In Michel, K. and Jobes, D. A. (2011). *Building a Therapeutic Alliance with the Suicidal Patient.* Washington, D.C.: American Psychological Association, pp. 206-208.

Jobes, D. A., and Ballard, E. (2011). The Therapist and The Suicidal Patient. In Michel, K. and Jobes, D. A. *Building a Therapeutic Alliance With the Suicidal Patient.* Washington, D.C.: American Psychological Association.

Joiner, T. E., Van Orden, K. A., Witte, T. K., and Rudd, M. D. (2009). *The Interpersonal Theory of Suicide: A Guidance for Working with Suicidal Clients.* Washington D.C.: The American Psychological Association Press.

Jung, C. G. (1959). The soul and death. In H. Feifel (ed.), *The Meaning of Death.* New York: McGraw-Hill, 1959.

Kernberg, O. (1975). *Borderline Conditions and Pathological Narcissism.* New York: Jason Aronson.

Kleitman, N., Phillip, A., Greer, S., and Bagley, C. (1969). Parasuicide. *British Journal of Psychiatry*, 115:746-747.

Klopfer, B. (1961). Suicide: The Jungian Point of View. In Farberow, N. and Shneidman, E. *The Cry for Help.* New York: McGraw-Hill, pp. 193-203.

Lester, D. (1990). *Understanding and Preventing Suicide.* Springfield, IL: Charles Thomas.

____ (2004). *Thinking About Suicide: Perspectives on Suicide.* New York: Nova Science Publishers Inc.

Levenson, E. (2016). *The Purloined Self.* New York: Routledge.

Litman, R.. (1967). Sigmund Freud on suicide. In Shneidman, E. (1967). *Essays in Self Destruction.* New Jersey: Jason Aronson, pp. 335f.

Maris, R. (1981) *Pathways to Suicide: A Survey of Self-Destructive Behaviors.* Baltimore: The Johns Hopkins University Press.

Menninger, K. (1933). Psychoanalytic Aspects of Suicide. *International Journal of Psycho-Analysis, 14*:376-390, Kindle version.

Michel, K., and Valach, L. (2011). The Narrative Interview with The Suicidal Patient. In Michel, K. and Jobes, D. A. *Building a Therapeutic Alliance with the Suicidal Patient.* Washington, D.C.: American Psychological Association, pp. 65-106.

Miller, J. (ed.) (1992). *On Suicide: Great Writers on the Ultimate Question.* San Francisco: Chronicle Books.

O'Carroll, P., Berman, A., Maris, R., Moscicki, E., Tanney, B., and Silverman, M. (1996). Beyond the tower of babel: A nomenclature for suicidality. *Suicide and Life-Threatening Behavior,* 26: 237-252, pp. 240-241.

Ogunlade, J. O. (1979). Personality characteristics related to susceptibility to behavioral contagion. *Social Behavior and Personality: An International Journal,* 7(2), 205.

Phillips, D. (1974). The influence of suggestion on suicide: Substantive and theoretical implications of the Werther effect. *American Sociological Review* 39:340-354, p. 349.

Plath, S. (2003). *The Collected Poems.* (Kindle Version).

_____ (2013). *The Bell Jar.* (Kindle Version).

Pope, K and Vasquez, J. (1991). *Ethics in Psychotherapy and Counseling: A Practical Guide for Psychologists.* San Francisco: Jossey-Bass.

Quinnett, P. G. (2012). *Suicide—The Forever Decision* (Kindle Version).

Robins, E., Murphy, G., Wilkinson, R., Gassner, S., and Kayes, J. (1996). Some Clinical Considerations in the Prevention of Suicide Based on a Study of One Hundred Thirty-Four Successful Suicides. In Maltsberger, J., and Goldblatt, M. (1996). *Essential Papers on Suicide.* New York: McGraw Hill, pp. 143f.

Rosenstein, H. (1972). Reconsidering Sylvia Plath. *Ms.* 1:44-57 (September, 1972).

Rudd, M. D. (2006). *The Assessment and Management of Suicidality.* Sarasota, FL: The Professional Resources Press.

Rudd, D. M., and Brown, G. K. (2011). A cognitive theory of suicide: Building hope. In Michel, K. and Jobes, D. A. *Building a Therapeutic Alliance with the Suicidal Patient.* Washington, D.C.: American Psychological Association.

Shneidman, E. (1967). *Essays in Self Destruction.* New Jersey: Jason Aronson.

___ (1998). *The Suicidal Mind.* (Kindle Version).

___ (2001). *Comprehending Suicide: Landmarks in 20th Century Suicidology.* Washington, D.C.: American Psychological Association Press

___ (2004). *Autopsy of a Suicidal Mind.* (Kindle version)

___ (2014). *Definition of Suicide.* (Kindle version).

Spaulding, J., Simpson, G., and Durkheim, E. (2005) *Suicide: A Study in Sociology (Routledge Classics),* (Kindle version).

Stern, D. N. (2003). *Unformulated Experience: From Dissociation to Imagination in Psychoanalysis.* New York: Routledge.

Stolorow, R., Atwood, G., and Lachman, F. (1980). *Psychoanalysis of Developmental Arrests.* New York: International Universities Press.

Styron, W. (1990). *Darkness Visible: Memoir of Madness.* New York: Random House.

Sullivan, H. S. (1970). *The Psychiatric Interview.* New York: Norton.

Webb, D. (2013). *Thinking about Suicide.* Ross-on-Wye, U.K.: PCCS.

Welch, B. L. (2000). *Reducing Your Suicide Liability.* Amityville, NY: American Professional Agency.

Wikipedia. (2018). Suicide in Switzerland, retrieved 1-1-18.

Williams, M. (1997/2014) *Cry of Pain: Understanding Suicide and the Suicidal Mind.* London: Piatkus.

Wise, T. L. (2003). *Waking Up: Climbing Through the Darkness.* Los Angeles: Pathfinder.

Yufit, kR., and Lester, D. (eds.). (2005). *Assessment, Treatment, and Prevention of Suicidal Behavior.* New York: Wiley.

About the Author

Lawrence Hedges, Ph.D., Psy.D., ABPP, began seeing patients in 1966 and completed his training in child psychoanalysis in 1973. Since that time his primary occupation has been training and supervising psychotherapists, individually and in groups, on their most difficult cases at the Listening Perspectives Study Center in Orange, California. Dr. Hedges was the Founding Director of the Newport Psychoanalytic Institute in 1983, where he continues to serve as a supervising and training analyst. Throughout his career, Dr. Hedges has provided continuing education courses for psychotherapists throughout the United States and abroad. He has consulted or served as expert witness on more than 400 complaints against psychotherapists in 20 states and has published 23 books on various topics of interest to psychoanalysts and psychoanalytic psychotherapists, three of which have received the Gradiva Award for the best psychoanalytic book of the year. During the 2009 centennial celebration of the International Psychoanalytic Association, his 1992 book, *Interpreting the Countertransference*, was named one of the key contributions in the relational track during the first century of psychoanalytics. In 2015 Dr. Hedges was distinguished by being awarded honorary membership in the American Psychoanalytic Association for his many contributions to psychoanalysis through the years.

Other Books Authored and Edited by Lawrence Hedges

Listening Perspectives in Psychotherapy (1983;
Revised Edition 2003; 40th Anniversary Edition 2022)

In a fresh and innovative format Hedges organizes an exhaustive overview of contemporary psychoanalytic and object relations theory and clinical practice. "In studying the Listening Perspectives of therapists, the author has identified himself with the idea that one must sometimes change the Listening Perspective and also the interpreting, responding perspective." –Rudolf Ekstein, Ph.D. Contributing therapists: Mary Cook, Susan Courtney, Charles Coverdale, Arlene Dorius, David Garland, Charles Margach, Jenna Riley, and Mary E. Walker. Now available in a 40th Anniversary edition, the book has become a classic in the field.

Interpreting the Countertransference (1992)

Hedges boldly studies countertransference as a critical tool for therapeutic understanding. "Hedges clearly and beautifully delineates the components and forms of countertransference and explicates the technique of carefully proffered countertransference informed interventions ... [He takes the view] that all countertransferences, no matter how much they belong to the analyst, are unconsciously evoked by the patient." –James Grotstein, M.D. Contributing therapists: Anthony Brailow, Karen K. Redding, and Howard Rogers. During the 2009 centennial celebrations of The International Psychoanalytic Association his 1992 book, Interpreting the Countertransference, was named one of the key contributions in the relational track during the first century of psychoanalytics.

In Search of the Lost Mother of Infancy (1994)

"Organizing transferences" in psychotherapy constitute a living memory of a person's earliest relatedness experiences and failures. Infant research and psychotherapeutic studies from the past two decades now make it possible to define for therapeutic analysis the manifestations of early contact traumas. A history and summary of the Listening Perspective approach to psychotherapy introduces the book. Contributing therapists: Bill Cone, Cecile Dillon, Francie Marais, Sandra Russell, Sabrina Salayz, Jacki Singer, Sean Stewart, Ruth Wimsatt, and Marina Young.

Remembering, Repeating, and Working Through Childhood Trauma:
  The Psychodynamics of Recovered Memories, Multiple Personality,
  Ritual Abuse, Incest, Molest, and Abduction (1994)

Infantile focal as well as strain trauma leave deep psychological scars that show up as symptoms and memories later in life. In psychotherapy people seek to process early experiences that lack ordinary pictoral and narrational representations through a variety of forms of transference and dissociative remembering such as multiple personality, dual relating, archetypal adventures, and false accusations against therapists or other emotionally significant people. "Lawrence Hedges makes a powerful and compelling argument for why traumatic memories recovered during psychotherapy need to be taken seriously. He shows us how and why these memories must be dealt with in thoughtful and responsible ways and not simply uncritically believed and used as tools for destruction." –Elizabeth F. Loftus, Ph.D. Nominated for Gradiva Best Book of the Year Award.

Working the Organizing Experience:
  Transforming Psychotic, Schizoid, and Autistic States (1994)

Hedges defines in a clear and impelling manner the most fundamental and treacherous transference phenomena, the emotional experiences retained from the first few months of life. Hedges describes the infant's attempts to reach out and form organizing connections to the interpersonal environment and how those attempts may have been ignored, thwarted, and/or rejected. He demonstrates how people live out these primitive transferences in everyday significant relationships and in the psychotherapy relationship. A critical history of psychotherapy with primitive transferences is contributed by James Grotstein and a case study is contributed by Frances Tustin.

Strategic Emotional Involvement:
Using the Countertransference in Psychotherapy (1996)

Following an overview of contemporary approaches to studying countertransference responsiveness, therapists tell moving stories of how their work came to involve them deeply, emotionally, and not always safely with clients. These comprehensive, intense, and honest reports are the first of their kind ever to be collected and published. Contributing therapists: Anthony Brailow, Suzanne Buchanan, Charles Coverdale, Carolyn Crawford, Jolyn Davidson, Jacqueline Gillespie, Ronald Hirz, Virginia Hunter, Gayle Trenberth, and Sally Turner-Miller.

Therapists at Risk:
Perils of the Intimacy of the Therapeutic Relationship (1997)

Lawrence E. Hedges, Robert Hilton, and Virginia Wink Hilton, long-time trainers of psychotherapists, join hands with attorney O. Brandt Caudill in this *tour de force* which explores the multitude of personal, ethical, and legal risks involved in achieving rewarding transformative connections in psychotherapy today. Relational intimacy is explored through such issues as touching, dualities in relationship, interfacing boundaries, sexuality, countertransference, recovered memories, primitive transferences, false accusations against therapists, and the critical importance of peer support and consultation. The authors clarify the many dynamic issues involved, suggest useful ways of managing the inherent dangers, and work to restore our confidence in and natural enjoyment of the psychotherapeutic process.

Facing the Challenge of Liability in Psychotherapy:
Practicing Defensively (2000, Revised 2017)

In this litigious age, all psychotherapists must protect themselves against the possibility of legal action; malpractice insurance is insufficient and does not begin to address the complexity and the enormity of this critical problem. In this book, Lawrence E. Hedges urges clinicians to practice defensively and provides a course of action that equips them to do so. After working with over a hundred psychotherapists and attorneys who have fought unwarranted legal and ethical complaints from clients, he has made the fruits of his work available to all therapists. In addition to identifying those patients prone to presenting legal problems, Dr. Hedges provides a series of consent forms (on the accompanying disk), a compelling rationale for using them, and a means of easily introducing them into clinical practice. This book is a wake-up call, a practical, clinically sound response to a frightening reality, and an absolute necessity for all therapists in practice today. Now available in a revised and updated edition. Gradiva Award Best Book of the Year.

Terrifying Transferences: Aftershocks of Childhood Trauma (2000)

There is a level of stark terror known to one degree or another by all human beings. It silently haunts our lives and occasionally surfaces in therapy. It is this deep-seated fear—often manifest in dreams or fantasies of dismemberment, mutilation, torture, abuse, insanity, rape, or death—that grips us with the terror of being lost forever in time and space or controlled by hostile forces stronger than ourselves. Whether the terror is felt by the client or by the therapist, it has a disorienting, fragmenting, crippling power. How we can look directly into the face of such terror, hold steady, and safely work it through is the subject of *Terrifying Transferences*. Contributing therapists: Linda Barnhurst, John Carter, Shirley Cox, Jolyn Davidson, Virginia Hunter, Michael Reyes, Audrey Seaton-Bacon, Sean Stewart, Gayle Trenberth, and Cynthia Wygal. Gradiva Award Best Book of the Year.

Sex in Psychotherapy: Sexuality, Passion, Love, and Desire in the Therapeutic Encounter (2010)

This book takes a psychodynamic approach to understanding recent technological and theoretical shifts in the field of psychotherapy. Hedges provides an expert overview and analysis of a wide variety of new perspectives on sex, sexuality, gender, and identity; new theories about sex's role in therapy; and new discoveries about the human brain and how it works. Therapists will value Hedges's unique insights into the role of sexuality in therapy, which are grounded in the author's studies of neurology, the history of sexuality, transference, resistance, and countertransference. Clinicians will also appreciate his provocative analyses of influential perspectives on sex, gender, and identity, and his lucid, concrete advice on the practice of therapeutic listening. This is an explosive work of tremendous imagination and scholarship. Hedges speaks the uncomfortable truth that psychotherapy today often reinforces the very paradigms that keep patients stuck in self-defeating, frustrating behavior. He sees sexuality as a vehicle for both therapists and patients to challenge what they think they know about the nature of self and intimacy. This book is a must-read for anyone interested in understanding 21st-century human beings—or in better understanding themselves and their sexuality.

Cross-Cultural Encounters: Bridging Worlds of Difference (2012)

This book is addressed to everyone who regularly encounters people from other cultural, ethnic, socioeconomic, linguistic, and ability groups. Its special focus, however, is aimed at counselors, therapists, and educators since their daily work so often involves highly personal cross-cultural interactive encounters. The running theme throughout the book is the importance of cultivating an attitude of tentative and curious humility and openness in the face of other cultural orientations. I owe a great debt to the many students, clients, and friends with diverse backgrounds who over the years have taught me how embedded I am in my own cultural biases. And who have helped me find ways of momentarily transcending those biases in order to bridge to an inspiring and illuminating intimate personal connection.

Overcoming Our Relationship Fears (2012)

We are all aware that chronic tension saps our energy and contributes to such modern maladies as high blood pressure and tension headaches, but few of us realize that this is caused by muscle constrictions that started as relationship fears in early childhood and live on in our minds and bodies. Overcoming Our Relationship Fears is a user-friendly roadmap for healing our relationships by dealing with our childhood fear reflexes. It is replete with relationship stories to illustrate each fear and how we individually express them. Dr. Hedges shows how to use our own built-in "Aliveness Monitor" to gauge our body's reaction to daily interactions and how they trigger our fears. Exercises in the book will help us release these life-threatening constrictions and reclaim our aliveness with ourselves and others.

Overcoming Our Relationship Fears: WORKBOOK (2013)

Developed to accompany Hedges's Overcoming Relationship Fears, this workbook contains a general introduction to the seven relationship fears that are a part of normal human development along with a series of exercises for individuals and couples who wish to learn to how to release their Body-Mind-Relationship fear reflexes. An Aliveness Journal is provided for charting the way these fears manifest in relationships and body maps to chart their location in each person's body.

The Relationship in Psychotherapy and Supervision (2013)

The sea-change in our understanding of neurobiology, infant research, and interpersonal/relational psychology over the past two decades makes clear that we are first and foremost a relational species. This finding has massive implications for the relational processes involved in teaching and supervising psychotherapy. Clinical theory and technique can be taught didactically. But relationship can only be learned through careful attention to the supervisory encounter itself. This advanced text surveys the psychodynamic and relational processes involved in psychotherapy and supervision.

Making Love Last: Creating and Maintaining Intimacy in Long-term Relationships (2013)

We have long known that physical and emotional intimacy diminish during the course of long-term relationships. This book deals with the questions, "Why romance fades over time?" And "What can we do about it?" Relational psychologists, neuropsychologists, and anthropologists have devoted the last two decades to the study of these questions with never before available research tools. It is now clear that we are genetically predisposed to search out intersubjective intimacy from birth but that cultural systems of child rearing seriously limit our possibilities for rewarding interpersonal relationships. Anthropological and neurological data suggests that over time we have been essentially a serially monogamous species with an extraordinary capacity for carving out new destinies for ourselves. How can we come to grips with our genetic and neurological heritage while simultaneously transcending our relational history in order to create and sustain exciting romance and nurturing love in long-term relationships? Making Love Last surveys research and theory suggesting that indeed we have the capacity and the means of achieving the lasting love we long for in our committed relationships.

Relational Interventions: Treating Borderline, Bipolar, Schizophrenic, Psychotic, and Characterological Personality Organization (2013)

Many clinicians dread working with individuals diagnosed as borderline, bipolar, schizophrenic, psychotic, and character disordered. Often labeled as "high risk" or "difficult", these relational problems and their interpersonal manifestations often require long and intense transformative therapy. In this book Dr. Hedges explains how to address the nature of personality organization in order to flow with—and eventually to enjoy—working at early developmental levels. Dr. Hedges speaks to the client's engagement/disengagement needs, using a relational process-oriented approach, so the therapist can gauge how much and what kind of therapy can be achieved at any point and time.

Facing Our Cumulative Developmental Traumas (2015)

It has now become clear that Cumulative Developmental Trauma is universal. That is, there is no way to grow up and walk the planet without being repeatedly swallowed up by emotional and relational demands from other people. When we become confused, frightened, and overwhelmed our conscious and unconscious minds seek remedies to deal with the situation. Unfortunately, many of the solutions developed in response to intrusive events turn into habitual fear reflexes that get in our way later in life, giving rise to post traumatic stress and relational inhibitions…. This book is about freeing ourselves from the cumulative effects of our life's many relational traumas and the after-effects of those traumas that continue to constrict our capacities for creative, spontaneous, and passionate living.

Relational Listening: A Handbook

Freud's singular stroke of genius can be simply stated: *When we engage with someone in an emotionally intimate relationship, the deep unconscious emotional/relational habits of both participants become interpersonally engaged and enacted thereby making them potentially available for notice, discussion, transformation, and expansion.*

This *Handbook* is the 20th book in a series edited and/or authored by Dr. Lawrence Hedges and surveys a massive clinical research project extending over 45 years and participated in by more than 400 psychotherapists in case conferences, reading groups and seminars at the Listening Perspectives Study Center and the Newport Psychoanalytic Institute in the Southern California area. The first book in the series, *Listening Perspectives in Psychotherapy* (1983), was widely praised for its comprehensive survey of 100 years of psychoanalytic studies and a 20th anniversary edition was published in 2003. But the important aspect of the book—that the studies were organized according to four different forms of relational listening according to different levels of developmental complexity—went largely unnoticed. Also generally unattended was the critical epistemological shift to perspectivalism which since that time has become better understood. The subsequent books participated in by numerous therapists expand and elaborate these *Relational Listening* perspectives for working clinicians. This *Handbook* provides not only a survey of the findings of the 45-year clinical research project but, more importantly, an overview of the seven developmental levels of relational listening that have consistently been found to provide enhanced psychotherapeutic engagement.

Terror in Psychotherapy: The New Zealand Lectures (2020)

Contemporary neuroscience, infant research, and relational psychotherapy make clear that we are a relational species—that our brain and neurological systems actually organize in the first year of life depending on the relationships that are and are not available. By the second year of life a symbiotic interaction, characterized by mutual affect regulation and mutual attachment experiences, is becoming established. In Terror in Psychotherapy, Dr. Lawrence Hedges demonstrates how trauma experienced during these "organizing" and "symbiotic" levels of relational development stimulate fear, anxiety, and terror that have consequences for later relationships—in extreme forms laying the foundation for suicide and homicide. A series of case vignettes illustrate how early relational intrusive trauma produce terror in transference and countertransference experiencing.

The Relational Approach in Psychotherapy: The China Lectures
(2023)

Although virtually all psychological theories and schools of thought now acknowledge the importance of the relationship in psychotherapy, the relationship itself is conceptualized in various ways. In this book, a ten-lecture series presented in ZhengDou, China as a continuing education program to hundreds of psychotherapists, Dr. Larry Hedges surveys a 50-year clinical research program into the nature of relationship based on the therapeutic experience of and contributions from over 400 practitioners.

www.ingramcontent.com/pod-product-compliance
Lightning Source LLC
Chambersburg PA
CBHW031505270326
41930CB00006B/267